Including Me

Josette Whiteley

ISBN 978-1-916838-10-9

Printed by Biddles Books Limited,
King's Lynn, Norfolk

Acknowledgements

I was introduced to Linda K by Helen M. Helen knew Linda would keep me on track and stop me from 'running on.' Linda became my right hand, my proof reader and I wish to thank her for her guidance and patience.

Louise introduced me to Nigel as he was willing to visit me at home. His interactions as a publisher helped me to shape what I wanted my book to look like. Thank you Nigel. Thank you to Jake M for the photo shoot and poster design for my book launch.

Tina was a central part of our family. I am forever grateful to those who helped motivate and care for her... her sisters, all her family, friends, colleagues and professionals. Too numerous to mention but all truly appreciated.

Last but by no means least I would like to thank my husband Tony who has been by my side every chapter of the way, always on hand to make coffees and give me moral support.

1

Finding Out

In the 1950's television was beginning to creep into more living rooms but not my family's, not yet.

We were moving away from the Pearl Carr and Teddy Johnson singers as more exciting stars emerged.

Elvis Presley was ascending in the USofA sending the girls crazy. We had Tommy Steele with his smiling face and guitar, but we hadn't reached the dizzy heights of the Beatles era. Not in the late 50's.

One person I remember was a crooner style singer, a cheerful chap called Max Bygraves. He would begin his act by singing songs with lyrics which now would be regarded as quaint, 'pink toothbrush', 'tulips from Amsterdam', 'you need hands', 'gilly gilly ossenfeffer', we never knew what that meant.

We used to go to a neighbours after church on a Sunday evening and watch their television when cheeky chap Max was on Sunday Night at the London Palladium. Half way through his oh so innocent songs he would pause, smile at us and say "wanna tell you a story".

We would all laugh into our tea and biscuits at the story and feel happy as we went home.

Now I'm going to tell you a story which might not have the feel good factor.

I might have called it 'a broken dream' or 'a time to be shattered', 'things ain't what they used to be' or 'two and two really do make four.' I may think of the title at the end, something may just pop into my head.

Once upon a time in 1959 there was a child mother and a child father and one Sunday afternoon they decided to take their baby daughter who was seven months old and named Christina (tiny Tina), for a walk, to show off the lovely new sun canopy which they had bought for her pram the day before.

In the 1950's prams and sun canopies were large and tiny Tina's canopy had a luxurious fringe around the edge, (because it was top of the range) which caught the warm gentle breeze as they walked along, a perfect day in May - not a day to be told a piece of shattering news.

Tina's eyes looked to be following the movement of the fringe.

The mild day had attracted many other walkers some of which we knew. One lady stopped us, admired the new canopy and then asked,

"Can she sit up yet?"

"Not quite" said child mum.

"She's only small," said child dad.

"Is she?", said 'forgotten name' lady - not seeming convinced, and added that so and so's baby only weighed 4lb and he could walk at 10 months.

Child dad started to move off quickly and then lit up a cigarette.

(That should have sent signals to the child mother because when her mum had put two and two together and made four she lit up her third cigarette of the day. She only ever had two, one after dinner and one after tea, it was her routine but the unfolding knowledge that her daughter, without any shadow of doubt, was pregnant and still at school and a grammar school at that, just made her light up. Was I more shocked at that?)

For many weeks now the child mummy had been aware that something was not right with the baby. Her concerns that tiny Tina didn't seem to be progressing as quickly as others of her age and younger, were quickly side stepped by the rest of the family. Always the same reply of 'well she was very small'.

This seemed to satisfy the child mother, bringing to a close an attempt to perhaps be told something she did not want to be told. Best to stay with the knowledge that the baby had been small and needed time to catch up, yes that was best. She put other thoughts right out of her mind and brought in the drying nappies.

Yes she still had a normal baby she was just small. That was right. Didn't need to know anything else don't know why she kept thinking about it.

But complacency and collusion may be coming to an end! Why? Because she had seen something which started stacking up the doubts again.

It was quite simple really, just a photograph of Tina with the child parents. She was facing to the side and her head wasn't straight. It had a lop sided look. It had a Jean Fletcher* look. And when the child mother saw this she laughed and said 'doesn't she look like Jean Fletcher'?

The grandma and granddad were indignant and said something like-

'Don't be ridiculous why would she look like JF?'

As if daring the child mother to say something which required an answer, but they both had a stricken look and so the child mother let it go again.

But although her doubts had reappeared she did not want the now illusion of the normal baby to disappear, not yet.

There was the tiniest of chances that tiny Tina was alright really. It was just the way the camera caught her. Child mum wasn't going to think about it today they were going out!

---

* Jean Fletcher was a Mongol (it is the 1950's) who lived with her parents near to me. During our childhood my friends and I would play with/ hide from /be spiteful to Jean.

If I was ever on my own with Jean, probably waiting for some more friends to come along, hopefully with a skipping rope, I would look at her and think she has got hands and all her fingers why is she a bit different to us?

When I became older and we were acting The Merchant of Venice at school and Shylock's speech began with, has not a Jew eyes ,ears, hands etc - I thought of JF.

Yes she has everything like us and she can turn the rope for us with her hands (and sometimes be allowed a little skip) until we got bored and went off.

Thinking about this with hindsight, she must have possessed (along with her extra chromosome) a talent for understanding body language and she would just stand watching us and wouldn't come with us unless she was asked.

I am not comfortable writing or remembering this but I was only a child, and these episodes did help me in the future to understand the other children when Tina was snubbed by them.

I was more involved with Jean than the other Headfield Roaders (where we lived) because my mum looked after Jean during the school holidays as her mum worked. There was only a normal school for her to go to in the 1940's.

Jean would dance around our kitchen shouting "clips, clips Niglel clips" telling my brother Nigel that we were going to have chips.

Nigel and I thought her antics and speech were hilarious and would be laughing and giggling until we were rebuked by our mum and we all shut up, including Jean, and ate the chips. (A rarity in our family in honour of our guest.)

My mum disapproved of Jean's dad as he went to the working men's club and came home drunk. I used to think that he drank because his daughter was a Mongol and if only his daughter was normal like my brother and me and our friends, then he wouldn't need to drink because my dad didn't.

Back to the beautiful day in May....

An opening suddenly appeared for child dad. They had just walked past a family with dad pushing a disabled child in a wheelchair.

In Yorkshire in the 1950's the terminology would have been, "summat wrong with 'im".

The child father asked the child mother what she would do if she had a child with summat wrong?

She said she didn't know and then she bravely said that yes she would cope adding "as long as it wasn't like Jean Fletcher."

This would not have been the answer child dad was looking for and that was the end of that attempt by him. But it made the odds stack more firmly against a 'normal baby' in the child mother's mind.

Is there ever a good season of the year to have to ask a question when the answer would break your dream?

Or give you a shattering time because really two and two do make four. And things would never be the same.

Wasn't that the song "Tell Me On A Sunday" about, picking the right time, or the one to cause the least amount of fallout?

It was going to be this beautiful day in May (it was Sunday) , I did not make a mental note of the date. It did not seem a necessary thing to do.

When the child mother and child father finally arrived back home the house was empty as the family had already gone to church. Sung evensong.

The child mother fed and bathed the tiny Tina, put her in her cot and sat on the candlewick bedspread arms on the top of the cot looking carefully at her. Child dad came in and sat next to her and she knew that on this day there would be no going back to the normal baby who was 'small that's all.'

She would have to ask the question, which by now actually she knew the answer even before she had asked, if Tina had something wrong with her, and felt the affirmative nod from the child dad.

The next question was more difficult,

"She's not like Jean Fletcher is she?"

Again the little nod which meant yes.

And so they sat and cried together and the child mother got more upset and kept saying,

"No she isn't. She can't be because we have just bought an expensive canopy for the pram."

Did the child mother think she wasn't worth it?

Yes the child mother did because for a fleeting moment she thought she would not buy her anything again…

because she wouldn't know what to buy someone who was like Jean Fletcher. Because now the normal baby….

had turned into the handicapped child and nothing would be the same again, the world in the child mother's …

head had tilted and the whole meaning of life had not swung in her favour. Things ain't what they used to be.

Thank you Max.

The child father began to sell the little daughter to the child mother with,

"look at her looking round and she's holding her rattle, she's only seven months she's not like JF."

And she wasn't, because she was the child mother's baby and she was already wrapped around her heart.

Then the family came back but the child mother and father never said that the child mother was now in the loop of knowing that she and the child father were the parents of a handicapped child.

Why didn't she rush to tell them when they came back?

Was it too much in one day to have to say, "Actually I have just been told today that I am the child mother of a handicapped child."

Some things you just have to keep to yourself, just a short time longer.

They were asked had they had a nice walk? Yes. Where did they go? Round the block including up the hill where the child mother went to have the tiny Tina weighed and receive the free orange juice and milk powder and where the vaccinations would take place.

Did the nurses at the clinic know she had summat wrong with 'er?

They never said except to tell the child mother that she would have to look after the baby. The child mother resented this advice but just thought it was because she, herself, was young.

The child mother escaped up to bed. But she did not sleep.

She shared the news the next morning when she was bouncing handicapped child on her lap and suddenly saw the grandma of the handicapped child watching with a look of profound sadness on her face, and the child mother just said she knew 'about Tina' and they cried together.

Very unusual for the grandma and the child mum to show all that emotion, and Tina just looked at them both as if to say what's the fuss.

And the day went on and the handicapped child's granddad came back from work, and then the handicapped child's uncle, and the grandma told them both that the child mother knew she had a handicapped child.

Everybody got emotional again but what a relief that the child mother did not resent her baby she would look after her and she would not be put away.

This passing on of the knowledge of the child parents not having a normal baby but one with 'summat wrong with 'er' was achieved without a consultation with a doctor, social worker, key worker, or a plan.

At the time it didn't seem to matter and the intrusion of a professional would have perhaps turned the acknowledgement into a circus.

It was a family time.

And then the wider family and the neighbours were included in the knowledge that the child parents had a child with summat wrong with 'er.

It must have been such a burden to bear for the dad and grandparents and even the uncle who was only 16, "when were they going to tell the child mother" she asked? They didn't

know. What a weight! Was it going to be a lifelong weight?

The news that the child parents had a backward child became common knowledge and lots of strange folklore began to circulate.

Had the child mother looked at herself in the mirror whilst 'carrying' (being pregnant) the baby, that was the favourite. Although she wasn't vain she must have at some time looked in the mirror. Doesn't everyone?

Could have been that. Had a black cat/man crossed in front of her, she can't remember, had she, this is a cracker, spilled the salt and not thrown it over her shoulder or the wrong shoulder. Bad luck!

Some said that they had known there was summat wrong with tiny Tina others feigned surprise and some just had not a clue but all agreed that child mother would have to look after her properly because, now comes the differentiation, either she had been chosen to have this child with summat wrong with her or she was being tested for her wrong doings - it was the late fifties and teenage pregnancy was not to be tolerated.

She had sinned but could be forgiven. She was on a pendulum swing twixt the virgin Mary, and the devil incarnate. Well what was a child mother to do? Just love her baby.

So she did and everything settled down and the pointed fingers began to look for other newer subjects as Tiny Tina's family began to settle into their new roles.

And that is the end of that story of the child mother finding out.

Things were never going to be what they used to be. Max did you know about this when you sang your song?

No of course you didn't, don't get above yourself Josette.

Mum, Josette with Tina in the garden of her Godfather, Kenneth. It is in Headfield Road, Dewsbury.

Finding out with dad, Terry. Dad was in the R.A.F. so moved around quite a lot.

2

Moving On

My memory was that it was always warm and sunny when I took Tina out in her pram with the luxurious fringe. I would walk down to the town, shop for a few groceries, visit the post office leaving baby and pram outside as that was de rigeur in 1960.

We did not have a car and so all trips within walking distance were on foot, unless the child dad could borrow the Daimler owned by an old gentleman who the dad's mother worked for. So from being a very young child Tina did have some experiences of grandeur!

The three of us, child dad and mum and the tiny Tina, moved out of child mum's family home into a very nice large upstairs flat of what had been a grand house. It was nice to have privacy and to give my family a break, but the outside stone steps made it difficult to manage the large pram. The agent assured me that he would help to take the pram down the steps because "the baby was handicapped and couldn't sit up and be put into a small push chair", alternatively we could keep it near the dustbins under cover. If the child dad was on a day shift (RAF Church Fenton) he would take the pram down and leave it by the dustbins and someone, agent, my dad, neighbour would drag it up for me and so it worked after a fashion.

The flat was situated at the other end of the town a bit too near the grammar school for my liking but I was able to visit my family by either walking all the way –about three miles, or when the tiny Tina had managed to sit better we sometimes used a small bucket style push chair which enabled us to struggle onto a bus.

"Can I 'elp yer luv" was a godsend sound.

"You tek the pram…eh dear is that yours?"

"Yes she's my baby"

"Well niver mind you get on wi' 'er and a'll bring pram"

"Thank you"

To get off the bus, hopefully the kind person would help again and wait until Tina was slotted into the pushchair, and then leave with the now familiar,

"Yer'll atter look after 'er ya knaw".

"Yeh a knaw thanks fer 'elping".

Yorkshire people were not known for hiding whatever had shocked/ surprised them and I learnt very early in Tina's life to accept this reaction. No point in "kicking against the pricks" as my dad used to say, and usually tiny Tina and myself could rise above it all. Although it sometimes felt kindly words were tinged with sadness and relief that Tina was not their baby.

One day when we were on a bus, my maths and needlework teacher, Miss Brearley, got on and we both looked at each other in surprise and embarrassment. I was immediately transported back to school, the classroom and the teacher's cold eyes looking at me, as once again I had not understood a concept and had been made to look foolish in front of the class. This time we were both vulnerable, me with the reason I had left school on my lap, and she probably because she wasn't behind her desk so it was a bit awkward. When I got up to stagger off I thought that the cold eyes were a bit watery. She did not instruct me in the child rearing of a disabled child as in 'yer'll atter look after er yer naw'. She just said "good luck" with a wintry smile and a sad look which was bearable. It was looks of distaste and horror which were not, but it was 1960! Anyway, I hope I said thank you.

We were still living in the 'up the stone steps' flat, when I devised a way of helping the now two year old Tina to walk. There was no physiotherapist to help, but every day after tea time, Tina would have her reins on with the long strap and like a puppet (even her little hands turned outwards)

she would bounce around. We would try to keep her upright and to help her to put one foot in front of the other and not to sit down. Was I doing the right thing? This was 1960 and one could have felt isolated but what you have never had you never missed, and anyway there is something to be said for trying yourself. Well eventually something clicked and she was walking! What had I done! For the next eight or nine years I had to be one handed, as Tina was always ready to dart off.

Tina's power to move quickly, even when just crawling, was demonstrated when I heard a loud crash when I was out of the room and I rushed in to find the TV on its side on the floor and shards of glass sticking out. Tina must have been shaking the table, which she did when she wanted it switched on, but had got out of the way and was safe at the other side of the room. Well done Tina for moving so quickly!*

The dad took the television back to the shop in the Daimler and said it had "just gone" and was (reluctantly) given another.

"Good job an all" was a saying of Tina's when she was much much older but it fits in here as a brand new series had been born, Coronation Street, and we were hooked. Tina and I would sit together before she went to bed to watch the drama unfold. She would even recognise the signature tune- Da da da da da daaa. She would join in the last 'daaa'. At this period in her life she was trying out sounds and in answer to "where's your daddy working?" she would attempt to say Church Fenton.

When my youngest grandson was trying out sounds I was reminded of Tina's efforts and it always makes me sad to think they never really knew each other as Tina's death was just before his first birthday.

During this time we went to Doncaster in the Daimler to see the dad's dad who had gone to live with relatives after deserting his family. He was a thoughtless, spoilt man and who appeared to be pleased to see us, but was not really bothered. He was a heavy smoker and there was a full ash tray of cigarette butts near to him. We turned away and the next thing Tina was eating a cigarette end! We tried desperately to get all the bits out of her mouth and then she was sick.

---

* Is that why mums leave the toilet door open?

I think that this incident shaped her strong dislike of cigarettes and in adult life she ruthlessly pursued and held to account anyone she knew with "smoking again!" in her loud voice, as the person concerned was trying to hold a cigarette behind their back.

Life was changing again and the next move was in the offing. When you are connected to the military as the child dad was, and you are told you are being posted then you have to move, no debating the decision, which is why we found ourselves moving to Germany.

And I am having another baby.

Up the 'Stone Steps Flat'. Growing up – she is looking at a magazine. What's changed?

3

To Germany

I had never had much of wild giddy time or enjoyed myself with any sort of carefree abandonment, just the odd boyfriend, and then I met the dad with the ensuing consequence. In 1958 it was almost impossible to have a child out of wedlock, especially if you were from a respectable middle class family, you would be letting so many people down and what would the neighbours say? You could not put your parents through all that. You had to do the decent thing, and because the child dad-to- be was so desperate to marry me, that was decided upon and I had just been manipulated into something that was going at some time to end in tears.*

Before the wedding could take place I had to go to confession.** The priest was a pompous arrogant person and I disliked him intensely, however he absolved me of my sins leaving the way clear for me to have a Christian marriage, so everyone was satisfied - apart from me. After the event and the honeymoon in Bridlington I went to bed, and on being seen by a doctor was told that it had been too quick a transition from a school girl to a married pregnant woman! Correct.

It was 1961 when the child dad was posted from RAF Church Fenton to RAF Wildenrath in Germany quite close to the Dutch border. It was

---

* How things have changed with regard to out of wedlock pregnancies in the ensuing years, it is now not newsworthy or a source of shame to the white British – although our Muslim neighbours may think differently.

** A few years later I was informed by my mum that the priest had stolen some silver from another church and tried to flog it at Sotheby's. I think the custodial sentence was five years. I wonder if he went to confession?

regarded as an accompanied tour so Tina and I would be going, and I had a premonition that this was going to be tough, as I had lived in the same area all of my sheltered short life.

I had not finished my education, no college/university or even a job, other than my Saturday job, working on a tinned food stall on the market for which I was paid £1 a day, plus having to dodge the boss with his groping fingers. It was the mid fifties and an accepted part of working in a confined space with a man who was out for what he could get, it wasn't worth complaining. (Over sixty years later and hearing about all the sex scandals of "celebs" I can understand the women who were unable to complain at the time.)

It might be good to get away, but some of my school friends were giving birth and it had been so nice to go out with other young mums to the park - not many other places to go to in the early 60's, no playgroups yet. Tina was totally accepted amongst these young women and they delighted in her progress. (I am sure again tinged with the relief that she wasn't their baby.)

So....I had a mentally handicapped child and, to the shock and horror of the neighbourhood, I was having another child.

"Will it be all right" I was repeatedly asked,

"I hope so" was all I could say.

Child dad had gone ahead, so Tina and I were off to our new life taken by car from dad's work place to the RAF station where we would catch our flight to Wildenrath. It was so sad to say goodbye to my family and friends, with only letters to keep us in touch, no mobile phones not even a house phone. Isn't skype a good idea? I wonder what Tina thought about not seeing Grandma and Granddad.

Moving on to Germany. Tina is sitting with her baby brother Mark.

4

Living in Germany

We arrived in Germany in late August, Tina was going to be three in the October, and on the day after her birthday I was going to be 21.

The flight took an hour and it was difficult to keep Tina occupied. We would have had picture books, but she wanted to explore and RAF people are used to being obeyed, 'sit down' would mean sit down now!

But eventually we arrived and were met by the child dad and his friend, who drove us to our new home. The dad did not seem overjoyed to see us, and it was a difficult journey as I felt we should be back at home.

We had to wait for a married quarter on the camp as we did not have enough points for one immediately, so we went to RAF 'approved' accommodation. There was nothing I liked about the flat, it was an annexe of the landlord's house and Tina was growing and walking and running, and in case she bolted the door had to be kept locked. Everything was strange and I wasn't prepared for such a difference, but here we were at the start of two years in a strange land just Tina and me, even the dad seemed alien as, in his three months alone, he had taken on a new persona leaving us in his mind far behind.

Why didn't you just go back home I may have been asked. I would not have been the first wife to do that. No. Better to have the baby first. Give it all a chance.

The landscape of this new 'home' was flat and uninteresting compared to Yorkshire's diverse scenery. I soon found out that the older folk were resentful and some openly hostile to us foreigners. It was only 16 years after the end of the 2nd world war, and harsh memories lingered especially if you had lost one or more of your relatives. And here were the enemy living in their houses, but changes were coming slowly and attitudes were beginning to thaw.

Many Germans were employed on the camps so some good relationships were being built, however we were getting stares and almost finger pointing, which seemed very personal. Was it at the dad in the smart blue uniform of a corporal, or the bulging tummy of the thin, pale faced mum? Most likely it was the mentally handicapped little girl making strange noises and trying to escape from a restraining hand. Did I really think that I could cope? It never crossed my mind. I just felt a deep sadness at being taken away from my previous life. In brief I was homesick.

Tina was beginning to be toilet trained and she would make a funny little click sound when she needed "to go", so she was not so far behind children of her own age in that respect. She had noticed that there were children playing opposite to our place and because she was showing her gregarious nature even at this young age, I used to walk across the road with her as she wanted to join in. Titters and then silence descended as we approached but, undaunted as ever, Tina had seen a little pram that she wanted to push, and very fortunately the mum of the owner asked her child in German of course, to let Tina have a turn.

It was a connection I have never forgotten and when the pram was returned to its owner, possibly after Tina had pushed it over tipping the baby doll and nice cover onto the floor, the mum gave Tina a biscuit. However when Tina started to eat the biscuit, the stares and titters from the children started again as Tina's tongue came out and moved backwards and forwards as she chewed, and the problem of the weak muscles in her throat meant her tongue seemed to press onto the roof of her mouth softening the biscuit ready for swallowing with a gulp. The mums looked embarrassed and spoke quickly to their children in German of course and I was reminded of dinner times with JF and my brother's and my titters and my mother's quick rebuke to us. Yes it does help to remember yourself as a child in a similar situation when your own tongue stayed in your mouth whilst your food was being masticated, and if you ate with your mouth open you would be corrected by one of your parents.

However that was the beginning of us being not only tolerated, but shyly smiled at, especially when Tina could say 'danke' in her own little way, and me thinking 'what can I give her to gently say weidersehen, oh I know I'll give her a biscuit'- the beginning of Tina's lifelong love of biscuits!

Tina was very active and did not seem to understand the phrase 'wait a minute', well she did know but chose to ignore it, because if she wanted to move she was like a bullet! So I became one handed most of the time, but if I was in a shop and had to get money out of my purse then Tina's hand had to be released, and if 'wait a minute' was ignored she would be out of the shop and I would be running after her as fast as I could go with a big tummy. I had tried reins on Tina when we were out, but she would just lift her feet off the ground and remain swinging! Too tricky in my late pregnant state. When we returned the shop keeper would sometimes be looking stoney faced as I had yet to pay for the shopping which would have still been on the counter. It felt like we were still regarded with suspicion.

Was it the fact that we were foreigners, or, to be more personal, our little girl who had 'summat wrong wi er por kid', and was often tipping over prams and pushing children – more of Tina's tricks. Was it retribution or am I being hard on myself? I desperately tried to keep my head up. It is always hard to be the odd one out, not only having little Tina but also struggling with the language and the food. It was always better to shop at the NAAFI, a reminder of home where you could buy English food, and it is not surprising to me that the foreigners in our country want their own food shops.

Making a good show in Germany was to sweep the outside of your house on Saturday afternoon ready for Sunday and your curtains at the front must always be pristine - it didn't seem to matter at the back. Quilts were used for bedding and I wanted a blanket!

It was the wrong decade for us to be there.

We were meeting other English people in Wassenberg and wasn't it nice to be able to speak to each other in our own language without hesitation? Many many years later I passed a couple of women in my home town who were, I think, saying goodbye to each other in their own language and I remembered the relief of 'thank god I can speak in English even though

I am in Germany'- can you blame the foreigners in our country who do the same?

We were gradually finding our way around this new regime, of course there was no mother and toddler or play group to attend, it was mum and Tina, a walk, and cup of tea with an English friend when the dad was at work. It was a drinking culture as alcohol and cigarettes were dirt cheap in the NAAFI and there was the temptation to linger after a shift had finished and in the catering section where the dad worked, the mess do's went on well into the night. What would I have done if I had gone into labour, no phone of course, but I am sure the neighbours would have rallied round, because the local folks were beginning to communicate with a smile and a nod.

We were visited by a SAAFA officer who checked whether I was managing to get to the hospital for my ante-natal checks? I was, but it would have been helpful if Tina could have gone to a play group but I must stop saying that because it was not going to happen. However the SAAFA officer was very helpful to us when the dad and his car collided with a tree and he was in hospital with a fractured pelvis, she arranged for my mum to fly out to look after Tina when I had the baby.

My mum, who had never ventured anywhere other than her own narrow territory by herself, had to fly over unaccompanied to be with us - secretly I think she enjoyed being the only woman on the plane to Dusseldorf which was full of business men! It was lovely to see her and it took some of the responsibility of Tina off my shoulders. Mum had a very good voice which she put to good use to sing nursery rhymes with Tina, who joined in at the end of each line leaving a note hanging e.g. half a pound of "tuppeny ricccce da da da treeeeka" do you get it? No TV of course unless your deutsch was good enough, so we made our own entertainment.

Tina was 3 years old now and my due date was roughly mid November. On the 2nd December it was my mum's 50th birthday and I thought it would be nice to go on a little trip to Roermond in Holland, even though I was 9 months and 2 weeks 'gone'. (I was going stir crazy). Mum was a bit apprehensive

"Just us three?"

"Yes mum we'll be fine".

Well yes we got on the bus, arrived, walked around, we must have gone into a café and then we went to find the bus! That was when our problems began......there was no bus. I tried not to show that I was getting into a state of panic as mum would have freaked out and she was well employed trotting after Tina who was having a walk about, the light was beginning to fade (December) and I was praying that all this would not start the baby off. Looking around in a helpless way, I suddenly noticed a car with the British forces number plate!! Well, I thought, at least the person will speak English and he did with a Welsh accent. I asked did he know if there was a bus to Wassenberg? He was politely answering my question but I didn't want to hear the negative answer.

"No there won't be one until Monday" he said. Monday!

"The ambulance is coming to take me to the hospital on Monday to have the baby I must be back when they arrive with my bag packed." I added.

I must have sounded a bit delirious, but he looked at my stomach then at Tina and finally my mum, and being a knight in the shining armour of an airman he asked if he could take us anywhere. I would have knelt and kissed his shiny shoes but I might not have got up so I asked if he could take us to Wassenberg. I was praying that mum did not say that we will be alright as she didn't like to be beholden to anyone, but this was an emergency so we all piled in. I hope the baby doesn't start to come in this spotless car was another little prayer. We gavc him profuse thanks and little Tina grunted something and waved goodbye (I don't think he knew what to make of her). That was over 50 years ago and I can still recall the hero of the hour.

The baby was born on the following Wednesday a dear little boy. 'Normal' would have been the label attached to him.

We flew back home with mum much to the SAAFA officer's displeasure as she thought that the baby was too young to fly, but it was getting close to Christmas and mum had not washed the step and window ledges (see at least in Yorkshire we are not so different to the German preparations.) My dad would not have known what to do! My intention was to stay but the dad came to take us back. Yes things would be better, he would have more time off, we would move to a different flat with a nice family, we'll get a married quarter soon etc etc.

The 2nd flat was much smaller, part of a family house with two smallish rooms and a tiny space which was called a kitchen, with a sink, cold tap and a little cooker. I can't remember having a bodily soak for the nine months we were there - Tina and baby bathed in a bowl and the dad on camp - there was a tiny living room and a bedroom into which the four of us were crammed.

The dry toilet in the back yard was shared with the whole family. In this back yard resided a large rat which scuttled around and a rabbit in a cage which was waiting to be dinner. Next to the yard was a cellar with a dodgy washing machine and boiler. I was able to do our washing in the dodgy machine, and its electrics must have been faulty because you had to remember to walk to the left side of the washer, If I forgot (and it was easy to do so when I had to bolt after Tina) and went to the right, then I got an electric shock.

When I was doing the washing, and remember I had a young baby and no disposable nappies, so it was fairly continuous, it was helpful if Tina had gone into Oma's room. This lady had only one room (not even the tiniest area for a kitchen) where she ate, slept, entertained and sewed to make ends meet. She was a disabled lady with one arm that stopped at her elbow in a tiny finger and the other was smaller than a normal arm with two fingers and a thumb, and a club foot which gave her a pronounced limp. She was widowed when her children were quite young and had to sew to keep the family together, which would have been during the war - I wonder if her husband was a soldier. She was a lovely, smiley lady who was very kind to us and when she told me that she did not know of the horrors of the concentration camps, I believed her.

It was good to listen and try to speak to Oma as she could not speak a word of English. Tina was still saying 'dande' (danke) and something that passed for weidersehen. In Oma's room she would not only have a biscuit but a buterbrote as well. If I got stuck with the conversation I would ask her daughter-in-law Hilde, who could speak a little English, to interpret. She, her husband and 5 children lived on the upper floor of the house and sometimes I would go upstairs for a chat both of us trying to make ourselves understood. Their living quarters seemed even more sparse and dismal than ours.

One night when I was visiting, Hilde got out some photographs of her family to show me. She pointed to one face and said that it was her brother and he had died in the war, she said the word scheisen. I thought that was the word for shit—and I was at a loss as to why she was saying it when we were talking about her brother who she had just told me was killed in the war. I was not following this now, it was all being lost in the translation. What was shit to do with dying in the war. She knew I had not understood as I had said schiesen? pronouncing the I first.

"Nein" she said "scheisen" and pretended that she had a gun and was aiming it at me.

"Was he a soldier?" I asked.

She looked rather shocked and said "No like Tina".

I thought again I am not following this. Why would he have been shot if he was like Tina? She gave me the photo to have another look. She then told me the story. Her brother was in a home for the 'mentally handicapped', then one day the soldiers went into the home and shot all the children.

That is the nearest I have been to the horrors of war, hearing from one person how her brother who had done no harm to anyone had been killed in such a way. She treasured her very old photographs and I found it incredibly moving. I suppose the mentally handicapped did not have a place in Hitler's warped vision for the fatherland, the Ayrian race could not be sullied by imperfection. Unbelievable or was it? Are we in the 21st century trying to make a perfect society not by shooting dead, but by gently trying to rid ourselves of the imperfect by the testing and scanning of pregnant women? After that I was quite relieved when Oma shouted up the stairs that the baby was crying. I left Hilde having another look at her photograph.

The worst thing about living in this flat was the dry toilet which stank. Thinking about it now over 50 years later, having to shake the contents of the baby's nappy into the said toilet trying desperately to hold your breath at the same time, was not in my, or anybody else's, best interest. I was often ill with sickness and diarrhoea and then Tina became ill and the doctor from the camp came out. After his visit, and within three weeks, we moved onto the camp.

The electrics in the cellar were still giving out shocks when we left. The rabbit had become the Easter bunny on a plate. The rat was still running around. No other English family stayed there again. I really missed the family, but not the toilet, and we often visited them and Oma spent the day with us when my mum and dad came for a holiday.

At the married quarter, an inventory is taken of all the items present in the property on arrival which are not your personal effects, and on departure the list is checked and any missing or damaged items are paid for out of the airman's salary, this process is called 'marching in' and 'marching out'! It was certainly more comfortable. We had 3 bedrooms a living room and a kitchen. We could hire a washing machine for one afternoon a week- no shocks! We could walk to the NAAFI, Tina on the edge of the pram, we met more people, some of whose children went to a nursery school, but not I'm afraid Tina who carried on staying with us singing songs. Elvis' popularity was rising and Tina was doing her own renditions of Jailhouse Rock. On the radio was the British Forces Network in Germany so you could keep in touch with all the latest news and music from England and it was all in English - hurrah.

This was quite a happy time for us, the living as the summertime song said was easy (well easier). Tina was making herself understood quite well, she happily ate and drank mostly unaided, and enjoyed her favourite game of pushing the baby over, for which she would be told off. He was walking nicely now and the summer of 1963 was pleasant. We had some nice friends both English (one a nurse on the camp who had her lunch with us most days) and German, (one of whom visited England with us when in that same summer we visited our families in Yorkshire.)

One has often heard people saying about having a crystal ball and looking into the future, might we have been able to change what we are doing to prevent some heartbreaking event, could we have appealed and said 'I do not want this to happen to my baby, please stop it from happening'?

No the lottery of life would have to run its course and that little beam of life after a very short illness, so short that the doctor had said the day before that there was nothing really wrong with him.

"It just isn't his day."

It was his last day. And that was it.

What does it feel like to be numb inside your own body. Have you collided with a truck which has squashed your heart and lungs? Ask anyone who has lost a child and it will be explained in differing ways but the excruciating pain will be the same and it will be there for ever. On second thoughts, don't ask, it is too intrusive.

On the outside of your body you will be able to function in a reasonable way to the relief of all around you who will mistakenly think that you have 'got over it'. You will laugh and smile and enjoy yourself throughout the years but then suddenly you hear a name (as in Misty Blue) and the little flicker laid inside you will turn into the flame of remembrance. I am not going to go into any more details because it is too painful, after 60 years it is still too painful.

We were summoned to see Wing Commander W, the chief doctor on the camp. Thinking now as I write this in 2013, was he softening us up in case we wanted an enquiry into the whole botched affair did he think we wanted some payment? No in answer to all that, we wanted our baby back and knowing that that was impossible, well I gritted my teeth when he told me that I was the best mother on the camp. And we left it like that. I wanted to be the worst mother and have my child back but he wouldn't have understood so I did not bother to say it.

I have learned to challenge medical decisions more if I feel that a wrong diagnosis is being made about my children, you sharpen up. But the ethos of the RAF is you are expected to do as you are told. Tell that to bereaved parents! This life, this forces mentality, it wasn't going to work for us and especially as there was a mentally handicapped child who shortly would be needing to go to school. Did you think I had forgotten Tina in all this sadness. She was very confused and kept asking as to where he was. What could I say? What could anyone say.

We went on leave back to England and we were able to go to the wedding of Audrey and Alan, known by us as A1 and A2, not that we wanted to go. It was only 2 weeks after the "event" but A1 and I had been friends for a long time and it would have been churlish not to go, and as I said, on the outside you don't look any different, thinner and paler perhaps.

We were posted back to England to RAF Marham around the time when the baby would have been two years old. It is not only names that make the flicker stronger, but also dates, and you can immediately be transported. In November of that year, 1963, President Kennedy was assassinated, so I am one of those persons who knew exactly where they were on that date. For me it did not override my own sadness, the person I could identify with was his mother.

So we are saying wiedersehen to Deutschland.

When people know I have lived in Germany or I even offer the information that I have and they say did I like it, did I have a good time? I just say yes. That should be enough for a casual enquiry.

Living and swinging in Germany. Are you falling asleep Tina? What is Mark chewing?

5

Providence Street Swaffham

We are at RAF Marham but not quite there yet. Of course we still did not have the required points to walk straight into a house, even though the dad was a corporal technician now, which meant his stripes had to be upside down.

We had a small old house, comprising of three small rooms running length ways down the house ending in the kitchen, which had a door leading to the outside and the toilet! This was a flushing toilet I have to add. The upstairs had one large bedroom and a small one. I am not sure if this is synonymous with the countryside, but did we have to have rats running over our heads in the roof space which was shared with the other houses in the terrace? I thought I had left all that behind in Germany. I also thought I had left a flat landscape behind as well but there it was again. I suppose you can't have an aerodrome on a hill. At least we were a bit closer to our roots.

It was with some trepidation as to what to expect with our baggage of sadness, but onwards and upwards, or true grit as the John Wayne film said!

And Tina, who had turned five, was ready for an education. We are now in 1964 (yes we are still swinging away in the 60's, well some are) and Tina, in retrospect, was lucky. Following her review with a Dr Applegate, Tina was pronounced unsuitable for a 'normal' education, which made her eligible to attend a school for the educationally sub normal - ESN. If anyone is wondering why I say she was lucky, I think this was the best experience for Tina as she learnt to stand on her own two feet by not having to be guarded by a teaching assistant, which she would have had in a mainstream school.

Children with Special Educational Needs in West Norfolk had been educated in a church hall in Albion St. in King's Lynn, which had been deemed unsuitable and dangerous for mainstream children, but the SEN children needed to go somewhere so it was alright for 'them' to remain there! Again Tina was lucky, as the new lovely school in Marsh Lane was built and officially opened just before we arrived on the scene.

Tina was to be transported to school by taxi with an escort and the school was at least 15 miles away so the round trip was at least 30 miles a day for five days a week. It always makes me smile, in a rueful sort of way, when parents who haven't a child with a disability complain that their child had to travel two miles to school! How the other half live! Tina travelled with other children in the catchment area and it was a good way of her making friends and influencing people. She would return and tell us stories about her fellow travellers but because her speech was not very clear and it was a new topic for us we had to try and guess, or if Tina was persisting I would have to say,

"Tina I'll ask the driver or Mrs (escort), and they'll explain to me. Because darling I can't understand what you are trying to tell me."

Tina accepted this, and the next day the story would be told and she would wave goodbye contented. (Probably the contents of someone's lunch box had been revealed.)

This was the first time that Tina had been separated from me (apart from the short stay in the hospital when the baby was born) and I did wonder if she would settle at school, but I need not have worried as she was in her element. With lots of new people, including children, to become friends with, she seemed to take the change in her stride.

And Tina was adapting well to this little town in Norfolk, and possibly the town was becoming used to her. She had already worked out where she could go for the odd biscuit! A very nice chatty lady had called out her name and that was it, bosom friends, she lived in a newer type development just two doors away and it was easy for Tina to just "pop in". There was also a swing park at the other end of the town and we would make that a very regular trip. Yes we were settling but because of the run down type of house we were in, it would be better if and when we were on the base.

For the first time in her life she was in contact with the paediatrician for regular checkups. It had been observed shortly after her birth that she had a congenital heart defect, i.e. a hole did not close when she was born - a reasonably easy operation to perform I am told - but not for Tina.

"Oh no mother, it would not be possible for Tina to have this type of operation it may kill her you know. She is too frail to cope with the anaesthetic!"

And that was it. I didn't like to say that I was not his mother.

It was not considered the norm in 1958 to ask for more information from a doctor, the decision was made and Tina would live with a heart with a hole in it. Her extremities were blue when she was cold but this gradually subsided as she got older and, unless she was ill, she seemed to have a normal colour until, nearing the end of her life, the symptoms returned.

The other problem Tina had was that her left eye turned quite noticeably. But of course when the question was asked,

"Could Tina have her eye corrected?" The answer was almost the same although it was a different doctor and the year was 1964,

"It would not be suitable for Tina to have an anaesthetic", he intoned. "She can see enough for her needs," he added.

Because Tina liked to sit on top of the television it was decided that she may need glasses. So off we went to the opticians and it was decided to try her with a pair just for watching the television.

"Can she read mother"?

"No not yet", again ignoring the presumption of being his mother.

The first time she was given the glasses to watch her favourite programme of the time (Crossroads with Meg Richardson) she expressed her displeasure by throwing them across the room. So that was that.

She was a happy girl and was managing to communicate quite well. When we went into the town there was always someone she knew to question, and if the person wasn't sure what had been said I would interpret. I decided that if I was natural about it then it put the other person at ease, and the next time we met the person concerned they would have the answer ready usually to…... 'Where's your husband/ what's his name/ how old is he etc?' you get the drift. As the years went on, Tina was still making the same enquiries of people she met and eventually her sisters would interpret as well. Don't make a big issue of it is my advice.

Well we spent the summer of 1964 in Swaffham. I was expecting another baby which was something for us all to look forward to, as was our next door neighbour who also rented as the husband was in the American military. They were a friendly young couple pleasant to Tina (that was now my benchmark for liking or disliking), and we shared the horror of the rats. I had been stuck in the toilet with one trapped in the door and the neighbour had found one in the bath!! Yes they were good neighbours to us all but heaven help us if we had been black. To them it didn't matter about Martin Luther King having a dream as black people were 'niggers'.

Over fifty years on I wonder if they have changed their minds! What would have been their reaction to 'Black Lives Matter'?

Living in Providence Street, Swaffham. Tina is wearing a smart blazer type jacket. She is starting at the Alderman School in King's Lynn

6

Oak Avenue RAF Marham

Our new house was very near to the guardroom with a swing park opposite, and there was a lounge, nice kitchen and three bedrooms with an inside flushing toilet and bathroom. She was getting accustomed to moving on, so Tina soon settled herself in and seemed to feel at home once the television had been installed. Crossroads was the programme she didn't like to miss, and it was a good way to get her to leave the swings when Crossroads was on.

Our part of Oak Avenue was brand new and all the people around us were moved in at the same time, so there we all were in our brand new properties and woe betide if anything was damaged! All the families had young children and Tina was well accepted by everyone. My condition had been noted but this time no one asked me if I hoped everything would be 'all right' although they might have thought it. At times I may have let something slip about the baby to a sympathetic ear, but when I went to the ante natal clinic I had to give all the details of my previous pregnancies. That was hard, but do you know, you become a sort of automaton and train yourself to answer as shortly as possible. It had to be precise for my sanity you see.

Back to Tina, and in September 1964 she was back to school in the taxi plus escort, greeting them like long lost friends. She was getting used to this new way of her life and it also gave me a bit of a breather in my pregnant state. When she came back home and it was still nice and light we would go over to the swings where she was well known now, and the older children would take her under their wing if I popped back home or they would bring her back in time for –you've guessed crossroads!!

One evening 6.30 she hadn't returned and I went over to get her, to be told that she had "gone back". I did panic, and after searching the immediate neighbours houses and no nobody had seen her, it was decided to go over to the guardroom and report her as missing. Well that started a huge ball rolling the dad was contacted in the mess (big do on that night so much work to be done) he came back looking annoyed and worried at the same time, and then the RAF police turned up and started a house to house search.

She was 'found' in a house near the swing park, where I suspect she had popped into before for a biscuit, and was watching, you've guessed, Crossroads on their television.

What a shock for the poor folks to have the police on their doorstep but I suppose like lots of people in Tina's life she had just popped into see, (we called it on the scrounge), once a favourite programme had started she was unmovable. We were so apologetic to everyone concerned and for once forces personnel, who were not known for their sense of humour, gave us a wry smile as they went back to their duties. When the dad went back to the mess it was brought up in conversation by one or two of the officers and I think they all felt quite sympathetic about what we were having to deal with!

As Tina got older she could recognise the absurdity of her obsession with the TV soaps, and smile (not laugh) about it. Until of course it was time for East Enders and she was not in front of a television - preferably her own.

Well now we are in the autumn and my pregnancy has become problematic, probably due to the stress of keeping up with Tina, whose disappearing act was not the last, but the police became stoical about Miss Swann's adventures. My blood pressure was too high and there were items in my samples that should not have been there.

"You must rest with your feet up" I was ordered.

I did as there were plenty of opportunities when Tina was at school. It was not all doom and gloom and I had a responsibility to the new little baby to be.

One Saturday in early December Tina wanted to go out into the back garden and I knew she could not escape and would come in at lunchtime as she was always ready for her meals. When I said that the dinner was ready I noticed that she couldn't move, she was stuck in her little red wellingtons in the mud! Out I went moaning, I am sure, and tried to move first one foot and then the other. She was well and truly stuck and instead of calling for some help which would have been more sensible I pulled her out by easing first one foot out of the boot and then the other. I could feel my head pounding rhythmically. This did not assist my blood pressure, I was diagnosed with toxaemia and was admitted to the RAF hospital in Ely for a week, and then sent home to rest. You may be pleased to know that Tina was taken by her dad to Yorkshire to stay with Grandma and Grandad and was brought back with them on Christmas Eve.

I was readmitted to hospital on the 27th and the dignified sister, as she will be known, was born on the 28th weighing only 5lb 1oz. She was born very quickly which did not give the midwives time enough to catch up on their Christmas activities 'is anyone paying attention to me' I could have said.

A dear little girl with a 'normal' diagnosis.

So Tina had a little sister, who, although she didn't know it then, was going to be an invaluable support to her older sister.

It is 1965 now and Tina is soon going to stop being a Mongol and start to be a person with Down's syndrome the name of the doctor in 1862 who discovered trisomy 21 and the extra chromosome. The society named the King's Lynn Society for Mentally Handicapped Children had come into being and the dad became the secretary of said society. The term' learning disability' had not yet replaced 'mentally handicapped', and for some reason Norfolk decided it would be 'difficulty' instead of 'disability'. Tina didn't seem affected by the change but I thought that Down's was more dignified.

We had one incident with the sister when she was about 14 months. I had called out the doctor one Saturday as she was very hot and I was not sure of the problem. He said it could be a teething problem and left saying she may have a seizure if her temperature kept rising. Well she did (have a seizure), a funny shout and then all limbs moving and shaking. Years later this information came very useful to us when Tina began to have seizures, but at this time I was absolutely terrified and ran out of the house calling for my neighbour to go and be with the dad as I was going to ring the doctor from the guardroom.

I raced back and the doctor did come, and he was chummy and cheerful and said to bring her to the surgery in a few days and he would give her a good examination, which we did and he pronounced her quite well.

A footnote to this was that during the panic, we had left the bottles sterilizing in a pan of water and the bottles had melted leaving huge streamers of black cobwebs and soot covering the kitchen! The kitchen had to be completely redecorated, tackled by some airmen who may have been on jankers, but they were very chirpy about it and in no time it was nearly pristine again. Remember the 'marching in' and 'marching out'? -we did get a bill, well not really a bill, but a slip to say money was to be deducted from the wages.

I am not sure how Tina greeted this incident when she arrived back in her taxi, but as her speech improved and vocabulary developed it would have been, 'Cor blimey mother you plonker' - but at only six years old she wasn't there yet.

In the years before parents' obsession with keeping their children safe, it was the done thing for children to play out and Tina loved to be out. It was hard work making sure she was where she should be, and if I was feeding the dignified sister then Tina had to wait, but she loved looking through her books and singing along to the radio whilst she was waiting to be let out. Tina had her favourites, like her grandma she liked the Rolling Stones, but the Swinging Blue Jeans and their hippy hippy shake got Tina shaking and singing away, and she enjoyed Top of the pops although at this time 1965/6 it was very much in its infancy.

The following 18 months after dignified sister's birth was a happy time at Marham and Tina certainly learned about life Tina style, like how to get the most out of people and I'm not just talking sweets and biscuits! However her pursuit of the latter led to her having lots of her baby teeth out when she was six. She was allowed an anaesthetic on this occasion, and hardly moaned at all after the procedure although her mouth must have been sore. "Cut down on the sweets and biscuits Tina", was the kindly advice. A slight hint to me I am sure, I didn't think it was appropriate for me to come clean about Tina's scrounging habits.

Information was what she required of everyone she met, starting with their family situation husband/wife/children how many/ home/ work/ car or bus/ television programmes/ shopping /meals. Tina's appetite was insatiable for this type of information which she would then come and divulge to us. Because her speech was not very clear it became a guessing game as Tina would not accept a nod or shake of the head or mmm as a satisfactory answer and if all else failed it had to be, 'I can't understand you.' She would accept this, but try your best to find out is my recommendation to anyone living with a child with a speech impediment.

Back to Marham with the dignified sister walking and enjoying the swing park, with Tina really settled and enjoying school life, and then came the news which all service folks become used to, which is a different posting. Some posts were unaccompanied, and this was one of them to Sharjah in the Persian Gulf.

If your husband is posted away from the camp the family is not allowed to remain in the house and other arrangements have to be made, so Tina, dignified sister and mum went back to Yorkshire. Tina had to say goodbye to all her new found friends on the camp and at the school, then we were off.

Living in Oak Avenue, R.A.F. Marham. Tina is now six years old and is with her baby sister Rachel who was born on the 28th December.

7

Back to Headfield Rd Dewsbury

It was strange to be back with your parents and to fit in with their routine. I had left as a very young naïve girl, even moving to the nice 'up the stone steps' flat was not a totally maturing experience, as family and friends were close by. That was left to the harrowing German experience of the baby's death with part of myself having died; how can you not become more life hardened by an episode of that magnitude in your still very young life?

Was I ready to face the Yorkshire form of inquisition? It started soon enough....

I was on the bus one day with the dignified sister and a neighbour of my parents struck up a conversation with me.

"Eeee Jorzet it wer awful t'hear 'baht yer baby we wor reight upset.

An ous this then? Yer a luvly lickle gurl ant ya, wot's yer name?"

With a bit of help from me and because dignified sister was a very good speaker the lady knew what she said.

"Ah that's a nice name" And she chatted on a bit more to the 'lickle gurl' asking her how long would she be staying at grandma and grandad's and "where's yer dad gone then?"

I had to help to answer that and then to explain about unaccompanied tours and no we couldn't stay in our house on the base and no I don't know where we will be going next which was true I did not.

On the back seat of the bus were some ladies clutching bags and purses going off to do their shopping I presumed. They had been chattering together until Winnie the neighbour started her interrogation of me and the dig sister. Silence fell and then one or the other would fill in the information to the ones not in the loop of my business.

'"What did she say about 'er baby'"

"He died when they were living in Germany"

"Eee that were sad for um."

"Yes it wor and the girl Winnie were asking about, she's got summat wrong wi er that's why she goes to that backward school in Savile Town."

"Oh yeah in Orchard St. Me neighbour were a cleaner there. She said they learn um to read and that."

"Aw that's nice."

Did these busy housewives know that I could hear all this? Oh well they weren't being judgmental. They just needed to know.

Winnie was concentrating on gleaning enough information from the dignified sister to be able to circulate on another bus trip, which was very satisfactory all round as dignified sister did not need much of an interpreter, and she chatted merrily away and I did not have to answer any more questions about the baby so he could be put back into the piece of my heart reserved for him.

What can you say? It was always well meaning and people did like to think you had 'got over it' and that you would not dissolve and scream and shout and say things like 'why me?' 'why my child?' What would have been the point. Nothing would change.

"Ows Tina gerring on. Is she at school now?" That question was definitely addressed to me

"Yes thank you she's very well and she's started at school in Orchard Street. She's eight years old now."

Well here we are in the bus station and we said our goodbyes to Winnie and the ladies who had been sitting on the back seat. As we walked off I noticed that they all huddled together probably to compare stories and fill in the gaps. Well that is what people do when a 'sheep returns to the fold' isn't it? Someone has to be first with the news.

I should have asked Winnie how Jean Fletcher is keeping. I must ask my mum.

Well Tina had started at Orchard Street school and to my shame I cannot remember how she got there. It was only a mile and a half away so was she picked up? When you are trying to go back into your past do you have a mental block on some issues? There is nobody to ask as all my family of the time have died, it was over fifty years ago. But we must continue and leave time to pass at its own speed.

Tina soon settled into the new school where her love of nearly everyone and nearly everything was reciprocated. She had actually made a visit to the school when she was still a babe in arms. Jean's mum had invited us to a concert and when the singing started I thought will my baby sound like that, baby Tina looked quite startled! It was such a loud raucous sound but everyone else was clapping and thoroughly enjoying the event so I tried to pretend that I had.

Experiences can help you to understand the feelings of others and throughout Tina's years in education when I have witnessed frozen faces on some guests at a concert, I don't get upset about it. If they come a second time they will be prepared!

Some of the staff remembered Tina from her first visit and were really pleased to think that she would be there for a whole year. I was prepared for the concerts and really enjoyed them. My mum and the dignified little sister came as well, little sister wanting to join in, and she did have a tuneful voice at her young age so when Three Blind Mice started she sang away and then did the actions to Humpty Dumpty including not pretending, but actually falling down, which was disruptive. My mum was a bit concerned and thought it might put the children's singing into the shade. I did agree but how can you explain that to a child who was not yet 2 years old.

The children, as in the Norfolk school, had the full range of disabilities associated with a moderate or severe mental handicap, (still a little more time before learning disability was the correct terminology). Folks with, (don't say suffer from), Down's syndrome (are we at this terminology yet in 1966?) have the particular problem because of their extra chromosome, of controlling the air flow from the lungs, and consequently the words either come out in a rush or there are long pauses for stuttering. Some folks with Down's have much clearer speech and I am so pleased for them but I'm afraid Tina was not fortunate in that respect as the roof of her mouth was not a rounded shape but almost going into a point.

Tina was not that keen on community singing even as a young girl, she would have been better employed at working the room and picking up all the information that was so necessary to her existence. When she attended the adult training centre roughly 15 years from this time a choir was formed there but Tina did not join.

"It's a load of crap" she would say as an explanation, "They can't sing".

Tina liked professional singers, the ones who made records and sang their latest on the television. Her favourite genre was always country and western Dolly Parton and Tammy Wynette types. When I said that she was being mean and it was very enjoyable to sing and the folks were enjoying the experience she just said,

"Well you can't". And I have had to live with that!

Back to 1966. Apart from the enforced singing Tina enjoyed her time there. She became very interested in jig-saw puzzles which, having to pick up and place pieces into position was so good for co-ordination and exercise for her fingers. It was also noticeable that dignified sister was going through the same stages of development and I must say working through them more speedily. She could dress and undress a doll, whereas Tina would just sling the doll across the room she was not interested in nurturing, and that would produce wails from the dignified sister. Tina could not manage a tricycle, whereas her sister in the spring after her 2nd birthday could ride reasonably well, so the gap was narrowing, and soon Tina began to fall behind her much younger sister in most skills. She was not aware of it so it did not, and never did give cause for concern and so they both moved along at their own speeds, colouring, forming letters, jigsaw puzzles, singing, and watching the tv.

At this stage of her life Tina just enjoyed the actual moment of whatever was happening, the television soaps were still favourite especially Crossroads and Coronation Street. We used to have concerts in the kitchen in the evening before bedtime with dignified sister and Tina pushing to see who went first. Tina was stronger and had a firm push, so she would be told off for pushing, and we would have to wait for the dignified sister to stop crying before we could begin the show in earnest. This type of concert became a family routine which lasted until my dad's, and then mum's deaths.

A firm favourite of Tina's and the dignified sister's was "Three wheels on my wagon" sung by the Christy Minstrels, and then the wheels began to drop off one by one and the singers on the wagon were having to escape from the Cherokee Indians! Tina was bored in the middle but dignified sister carried on until it was finished, with Tina perhaps filling in with "gapping by" "wollingonnnn" Tina speak for 'galloping by' and 'rolling along'. Mum would sing our favourite Yiddisher Mama, and we would all join in with her and then back to the Nursery rhymes before bed. The three of us slept in the room which had been mine before my brother took it over, but he had to go back to the box room for the duration of our visit.

In the August of 1966 we went on a holiday to Llandudno with mum and dad, staying in a bed breakfast with evening meal. Mum would have hated having to eat a cooked meal in the evening- not good to go to bed on- and it must have been tough having to help me with the children, not much of a holiday by the sound of it but we thought we had had a good time. We managed to get Tina onto a donkey but as usual her balance was not great and she slipped so far off the centre that I was carrying her top half most of the way. Tina was always enthusiastic to try something and then usually came a cropper but she was satisfied that she had tried and in her usual chirpy way would often say 'Iwentonadon key dinti mum!' To which I would reply 'do you want to do it again?' And she would say emphatically "no I don't", and from that time onwards she has never shown any enthusiasm for donkeys or horses!

Tina's godmother and her husband Audrey(A1) and Alan (2)were living quite close as A2 was studying at bible college and A1 was working as a consultant's secretary, she was totally self taught as she had to leave school at 15 and bring some money into the house. Their first child, a boy, was a month older than the dignified sister. A1's sister who lived with them also had a young child, so looked after both the children whilst A1 worked. Why am I saying all this? Because they were very important in, not only Tina's life but all my family's life, and will feature again and again.

Well we used to walk to see them occasionally, sometimes just dignified sister and myself giving my mum a break, but at other times, Tina, and sometimes mum and dad and me would all walk around the area where my dad had been born, now over 100 years ago, at the local shop run by his mum.* We walked a lot as dad had never driven, mum would have never ever thought that her place was behind the wheel of a car, and I was still a few years off driving myself.

Tina, dignified sister and myself, would visit the dad's mum and his younger siblings who had moved to the other side of the town, and I was in contact with my old school friends, some had made better choices of husbands than others and all had children. So once they thought that I had got over the baby's death we could all carry on as before I went to Germany.

In the new year 1967 the dad came home on leave and we went to London staying with people we had made friends with in Germany. The day was very exciting until poor little dignified sister fell over and cut her head on a kerb stone, she was singing three wheels on my wagon at the time. We went by taxi to the nearest hospital, Tina enjoying this ride and dignified sister carrying on singing up to the point when the doc started stitching and then the singing turned to screaming. Tina was upset and joined in the crying. We were all in the room together, but it was soon finished and when the poor little girl was lifted up I noticed that the contents of her nose were left on the sheet which she had to put her face on. Nobody seemed to mind and she started to sing again which made Tina happy as well.

---

* Recently I have made two visits to, what will always be to me, "my grandma's shop". A1 came with me and we were greeted so warmly by Mohammed who appeared not the slightest phased by two elderly white women appearing in his shop, which is positioned across the road from the biggest mosque in Europe, and he gave us both a shawl as a present.

During this break we did both decide that the military way of life was not the best for Tina's education and because we had no intention of "putting her away", the dad said that he was going to try for a compassionate discharge from the RAF and apply for a job at the college where he had been working some hours whilst at Marham. All this was successfully achieved, and he was told he would be missed as he was to have been promoted to sergeant. So the upshot was, he returned from Sharjah, had an interview at the college, and we found ourselves once again on the way to Norfolk.

Our Yorkshire year went very quickly once we had settled to the routine, and it was sad to leave Yorkshire and the family and friends and the Orchard St School.*

Just before leaving Yorkshire I found out that I was having another baby.

* The school in Orchard Street is now an Islamic centre.

Back to Headfield Road, Dewsbury. On holiday in Llandudno in 1966 and Tina was now eight years old. Is Tina laughing or crying? She had fallen on the jetty and hurt herself.

8

St. Edmundsbury Road North Lynn

In August of 1967 we arrived in St Ed's Road to a council maisonette. On appointment to his job at Kings Lynn College, the dad went straight to the council and secured us a home for a shortish period until we had the money for a deposit on a house. Because the dad was regarded as a key worker we were given the maisonette but at a special price - we had to pay £1 a week extra for jumping up the queue. I was becoming accustomed to arriving at a property that I had never seen before and making it mine and my family's home, and I was relieved to find a ground floor maisonette, Tina's disability did open some doors.

We had travelled in a removal van which my brother had driven, and I am thinking did we have all the furniture for our existence, as we had been accustomed to living in furnished houses and flats? Well there most certainly was 'stuff' in the van as we made numerous trips from the roadside to the front door. A quick call to Gloria, a great friend from those days, reminded me "you did not have anything so he, the dad, went and bought it all", including the gold carpet he was vacuuming on our arrival.

These trips from van to front door were accompanied by, what is referred to now, as a 'domestic', being played out in the flat above ours. I was becoming embarrassed, my children, brother plus girl friend, and I think Tina's godfather, or was it uncle Brian, who had come as well, could all hear the words that even living the life of forces personnel I had not encountered before. Where have we come to now I thought, is this what life is going to be like in Norfolk? If that type of argument had happened on Marham camp the family officer would have made a visit like sharpish!

"By 'eck ar kid y've cum to a reight doss ere!" said my brother.

"Well it might not be that bad, don't tell mum and dad." I replied, which meant of course that he would, but they would come and see us soon and judge for themselves.

Back to the Saturday in August 1967:

What is Tina doing whilst we are backwards and forwarding? She had come through the front door into the lounge, through the hall, and then straight out the back door to the communal area for hanging washing, access to the dustbins and where children could play out! She had already started her meeting and greeting tactics, making friends and influencing people. This time it was a small elderly lady with a pronounced limp who reminded me of Oma in Germany and, although she obviously spoke English, I still could not understand her very well as she had a very distinctive North Lynn accent!

Tina had taken her open door as a welcome to herself and was coming out with a......guess what?, with the lady saying that she thought her mother would be looking for her, and that she could come again if she was living 'ner herr.' I introduced myself and said that we were moving in, and all this time the domestic was rumbling on upstairs, which must now have moved to their back rooms. The little lady seemed oblivious and I dare not comment in case she was a relative. I introduced her to the dignified sister and she was also invited round and was complimented on her speech.

"Don't she talk well" she remarked.

She never told us what her name was and I came to understand that some (I had better say) Norfolk people do not introduce themselves immediately on meeting someone new, and dare I say foreign, to them. They play it safe rather than immediately committing themselves to a friendship. I was known as 'Tina's mum' throughout all our years together, and some folks just found my name too foreign and so they stuck to what they knew, that I was Tina's mum.

It was sad to see my brother plus girlfriend, and the godfather - or was it uncle Brian? - leaving, and I had to once again start living without my extended family, but it was all 'doable' so 'onwards and upwards'.

It was the summer break so Tina had to wait before renewing her friendships at the Alderman Jackson school she had attended a year before and the little dignified sister was going to start at a playgroup for 2 mornings a week.

In the interim friendships and acquaintanceships were beginning to be formed. Everyone in the near vicinity of the large yard outside the back door, became used to Tina's presence and she learnt which of the neighbours were the best to pop in and see for a snack.

"Allo Teener r yer allroight"

This became a familiar sound to which Tina would often reply,

"Whatsyourname", leaving the person concerned that Tina had momentarily forgotten her name and then a guessing game began to take place.

"Yew know wot moi noime is!"

Well no she didn't and neither did I. So when Tina looked at me and said,

"Mum wasshername?"

I would just looked blank and then the dear little dignified sister would say it. Hooray! She would often be around Tina when she was collecting information and helped out with translation, although at this time she was not quite three. Tina was unconcerned about how someone, six years younger than herself, could be her translator, that problem became more apparent as she grew older. Now a much longer broken conversation could take place. The person concerned had to run through who she was married to, number of children she had plus names, what she did for work and then probably excusing herself as she was going to be late for work.

Unlike my home town of Dewsbury where many of the women worked in the mills, in Norfolk they did agricultural field work or worked on production lines in the canning industry, often part time in the evenings so husbands and occasionally neighbours would care for their children.

Gloria was one of these workers, and a plus for friends and family was that we could share in the buying of soup and meatballs. These became part of the standard diet for us North Lynners and beyond.

Nobody seemed to have money to spare within the maisonette complex, but there was always food to go round and we would lend each other food items or money, 'just till I get paid please', if there was too much of the week left. I was always conscious that Tina may have raided someone's fridge or cupboard, what about the sandwiches I had seen her scoffing on the evenings of the running around times, perhaps they had been sitting on a table waiting for the would be recipient to return home….to an empty plate? So I was pleased to help out and I think the dad's salary may have been higher than many of the dock workers. Clothes, prams and push chairs, cots and toys, were all passed between neighbours. There was real support and no child went to school hungry, even the ones who could not get up early would get out their child's breakfast the night before, I am thinking of Gloria! There were some children who slipped through the net but Gloria helped a lot of them, there were quite a few staying with her, and two of her daughters have carried on the family tradition of being carers.

Well the month of August was coming to a close and the college and Alderman Jackson school would soon be starting back. I did not know who to contact re Tina starting school but because her friend Wendy (from before we went back to Yorkshire) lived just diagonally opposite to us, I thought it would be a good idea if Tina hitched a ride on her transport. I went to see Wendy and her mum and told them of my plan. After all I reasoned I didn't have a car and couldn't drive anyway, the dad was starting a new job etc, I had the dignified sister and I was having another baby what could be the harm? Wendy's mum didn't look too happy about the arrangement but she didn't protest too much as she could see my predicament.

Wendy was the youngest of seven children and she and Tina were the exact opposite to each other. Wendy was slight, dark haired and had much better speech control than Tina who was, heavier, fairer haired, but more street wise than Wendy, who was quite happy to keep alongside her mum or sibling when they were out, whereas Tina could not wait to escape from us! I sometimes envied Wendy having older siblings, on Tina's behalf, however her personality would not have flourished in the same way and she did like to say "I'm the oldest y'know."

If Tina went to play in Wendy's garden she would find a way out and come back, much to the consternation of the mum but Tina could not be contained. They were such different characters and I am always slightly irritated when people will insist on thinking that all folks with Downs look, think and talk alike. There are some similarities but 'they' have different dreams hopes and aspirations and it is the responsibility of family friends and professionals to try their hardest to make sure that these can be fulfilled, or at least a more realistic goal could be aimed at and encouraged. Tina thought she could do and be anything, swimmer, cook model (she did very well at the first two but not until she was much older). The biggest difference between them was Wendy was cautious and would think an issue through, while Tina, in her impetuous way would jump in to whatever and usually 'crashland.'

"Think about it first Tina" was often said to her and she started to reply with,

"Don't be daft" which became one of her famous one liners.

Another door Tina would wander over to and let herself into was Gloria's, and if no one was about she would go upstairs and sit on Gloria's bed until she awoke. One day, when we were most probably knocking on all the doors to see where she was, Tina appeared out of G's door looking sheepish as she had been told to come back later when they were up. I reminded Gloria of this occasion and she said it was one of many. She also recounted how Tina would sit on her living room carpet and look through all her children's comics and no amount of -

"Tina can you pick them up now please I want to vacuum the carpet" was effective, as Tina, who would never accelerate her pace, went through each one slowly and methodically. So Gloria probably had to have another cigarette to stop herself getting irritable as she did like children to respond immediately!

Tina was continuing her friendship with Gracie, and when we went to hang out the washing, I would watch her wander along to Gracie's house and either go in if the door was open, or bang on it if it was shut. Sometimes it opened and if not Tina would drift back, and if other children were outside she would wander over to them and I would always check that she was being acknowledged and allowed to be with them. She would have her little bike, and learned to share by allowing another child to ride on it, but if no refreshments were forthcoming she would wander inside. If dignified sister was outside then I would have to stay near the door to watch her, while Tina was most likely helping herself to something tasty from the fridge, perhaps a sausage or a piece of chicken. I wonder again if Tina looked in other peoples' fridges? Nobody ever said if she did.

One little upset she had was when she was intending to walk into someone's house and the child did not want her in and slammed the door catching Tina's thumb in the door jamb. Tina didn't make it too much of an issue but the child concerned started screaming and so doors were opening to see what was happening and there was poor Tina with a bleeding thumb. It was a good job that it was Saturday and the dad was at home and was able to take her to the hospital in the car. They returned about three hours later, Tina with three stitches a bandage and a lollipop, which upset the dignified sister.

Please readers do not think that Tina was always left to her own devices. Every evening after tea there was usually a game of running round the yard out through the gate around the front of the block and back through the other gate into the yard again. Tina was in her element and it was a good bit of exercise after a biscuit or two had been scrounged. I, sometimes the dad, would be at the front window, yes I can see her, then at the back door to see her in the yard, the only time I went out was to give her a piece of toilet paper to wipe her nose. She was in her element and it would have been cruel to curtail her fun.

Well on the morning of school starting the dignified sister and I stood by Wendy's gate with Tina and waited for the mini bus, fortunately there was a seat for Tina although we did not know the driver or the escort, but I explained that Tina had been to the school before and that 'they' knew she was back in this area. She was reluctantly accepted on the bus by the driver and escort, well she had already got on, and then Wendy arrived and they were off. If there were times to be pleased about not having a phone at home, then this was one of those days.

Tina returned home, on the bus, with a letter - she wasn't registered, she hadn't seen Dr A, hadn't had a review, they weren't expecting her and she couldn't come for the rest of the week! But grudgingly it was agreed that she could attend from the following Monday when the paper work should be in order, and the mini bus would stop outside our door we did not have to bother Mrs Nobbs! Well that was a good start back to education in Norfolk, the word exclusion comes to mind, or am I being too harsh on the system? Many years later when I worked in a mainstream school which also had children with disabilities, another mother had done the same thing for her son with Down's. The deputy head was appalled as the proper procedure had not been adhered to. I chose to remain silent!

Once Tina was safely in school, I had to make an appointment to register with the GP practice for ante natal care. The dignified sister and I set off around the corner to get the bus into the town. The bus was late and of course I was about 15 minutes late for my appointment. After booking in and apologising, I was told that the doctor would not see me, I protested but he was unrelenting. I never saw him, all this was being relayed via the receptionist, but I stood my ground and explained about the toxaemia I had had and wanted to have this appointment as I did not want anything to go wrong. Back came the receptionist and said that a nurse would check my sample and it was clear. I had been put into a situation that was not of my making, perhaps it was retribution for sneaking Tina onto the bus for school! So you see Tina it wasn't only you who was discriminated against.

Apart from these brushes with professionals we were beginning to have a really happy time in the maisonette, however we were always mindful of the fact that this was a temporary home. The dad got himself an extra job as a taxi driver so as to speed up the saving for the deposit on our house, as we were on a limited contract with the council maisonette.

And so it went on, Tina continuing her education at AJ's and she seemed to enjoy all the camaraderie and would come home talking about other pupils, teaching and support workers, office staff and the cleaners, yes Tina was all embracing in her friendships.

Tina was required to see a paediatrician on a yearly basis, and these reviews took place in the main hospital long before the children's centre was built. The doctor had a measured approach to all his questions and seemed satisfied with my answers but fielded my questions as to Tina's heart and eye.

"Should Tina have had heart surgery Dr R.?"

"From what you have just told me Mrs Swann, all that running around in the yard did you say? She seems to be managing very well."

At least he didn't call me mother.

"How do we know if the turn in her eye is damaging her vision?"

"I think she needs to see an optician. He may decide that she needs glasses."

Not another pair of glasses to be chucked across the room I thought but did not bother to say this out loud.

Dr R. was onto a different topic now so I had to put the probability of glasses out of my mind.

"Christina can you hop onto the scale for me?"

I had to give Tina a nudge as she only got her full name in a hospital situation and she did not relate to it. She slithered slowly off my lap and hovered with one foot off the ground and then proceeded to hop towards the scale. As she approached she paused and the other foot went down. She came back to me and started again. This time she had managed to reach the end of her hops but had not made it onto the scale, who would? Dr R, the nurse and myself, were watching in silence as Tina had taken his instruction at its most literal. I was the first to speak,

"Tina just walk to the scale you don't have to hop to it."

We all smiled including Dr R, that made us all relax and I am sure that Dr R made a mental note to himself to speak in a more direct form leaving no chance of misunderstanding.

And the dignified sister, what is happening at the play group? Before she began we had to go and see Sheila who only lived diagonally opposite to us, as she ran the play group sessions. I am sure most people are aware of the phrase 'if you want anything doing ask a busy woman' and this was the woman who epitomised the phrase! We were invited into this house and introduced ourselves, and Sheila and I became close friends.

It turned out very well. Sheila had worked at the school in Albion Street, (remember the one which was unsuitable for 'normal' children), after it had become available for handicapped children, and it transpired that Sheila had already met Tina. One day she suddenly turned around in her living room and Tina was standing there.

"Hello I'm Tina, wassyourname" said Tina.

Everything turned out fine at the play group, dignified sister found some little girls to play with, one of which was Gloria's younger daughter having already become friends with her in the yard. I admired Sheila for taking on the running of a play group with her own large family to look after, not to mention all the sewing and knitting she took on.

My pregnancy was progressing well, but I made sure that I saw a different doctor from the one I should have seen on my first visit. The midwife kept saying that the baby was small, and I replied that all my babies were small.

Mum and Dad came down for their first visit in October to coincide with Tina's ninth birthday and my twenty-seventh. It was lovely to see them and they thought the maisonette was very nice until "you get your own place" they added. "It will be nice to have your own garden". They didn't think much to the yard, although my dad was very sociable and when he was on duty watching the children he would chat away to whoever passed by. My mum was much more reserved and the dignified sister has her personality, but it is apparent that Tina's personality came from myself, my dad and grandma, after all a person with Down's has just one extra chromosome, the other 28 are from the mother and father.* We all had a lovely time together and felt quite sad when Mum and Dad had to

---

* Sometimes I think of Tina's life as a bridge between the haves and the have-nots, one little chromosome need not be a bridge too far need it? Surely the two sides could join up, and share understanding of the haves with their heart, eye, speech, movement that has been skewed by the invisible chromosome on trisomy 21. In total 47 not 46. When I wanted to write something before Tina died I thought of the plot being a society where it was an offence to carry an extra chromosome, and the person would have to go on trial for having this offending item on their person as it was to be outlawed! Is that so far from society's idea of perfection now?

go back, Dad to his job as the sales manager for a wagon works company and mum to her cleaning duties in the home and all her voluntary jobs.

In the autumn Tina developed a cough, but it was difficult to keep her in when the other children were playing, and as she passed the window I was horrified to see her face and hands a deep purple, and she immediately went to hospital where she stayed for a few days. I always remember the words on the discharge paper for the doctor 'Renal Collapse'. Nobody wanted to explain this to me and because she made a good recovery I stopped asking. This was over 50 years ago and doctors and nurses were not as into sharing information as they are now. This was Tina's first time as a hospital inpatient.

We had Christmas of 1967 in Yorkshire with mum and dad, the uncle, girl friend who is now fiancée, and saw lots of the dad's family. It was a happy time and busy, and I know we would have all gathered around the television to watch Morecambe and Wise Christmas Special. When the show had finished my mum, who was a brilliant mimic, would take us through the whole show again. Then it was back to Norfolk for the start of the spring term at the college, AJ,s and the play group and for me to wait for the new baby to arrive in two months time.

The month of March 1968 came and I was still being told that the baby was small and I was still saying all my babies were small but I was worried if would the baby be 'all right'. All mothers hope for this but it was an extra pressure for me knowing my history - but lightning doesn't strike twice does it? We shall see.

The day before this little one should be arriving, things started to kick off. It was Monday morning, the dad had gone to work, Tina had gone to school and the little dignified sister and I were hanging out the washing. Gloria looked out of her kitchen window and asked if I was all right. When I told her how I was, she came round and asked if I had packed my bag.

"Not yet" I said, "I haven't got all the things ready".

She disappeared for a bit and came back with her cigarettes and another nice neighbour who was given the task of sewing the buttons on my dressing gown.

“When were you thinking of getting everything ready?” she asked.

“Well it’s not due today” I replied.

She did not even credit that statement with an answer, but just announced that she was going to ring the dad and that would not be a five minute job as the phone box was around the corner by the bus stop. I bet she was praying that it had not been vandalised. The dad came, just as my helpers were getting apprehensive, saying ‘he had to sort something out’ which translated to having a swiftish half. We drove past Sheila’s house and saw her hanging out her washing her children tumbling around, she shouted at me to ‘have a boy’, and then we soon arrived at the maternity unit which was set apart from the general hospital.

Two hours later a tiny 4lb 9oz bird like girl with huge dark eyes arrived - sorry Sheila. The eyes were all I could see when she was given to me, and when I asked if she was ‘all right’ I was told yes in an off hand way. Her weight was commented on -

“Do you smoke?” asked one of the junior midwives who then seemed disappointed when I replied that I had never smoked. No other explanations were asked for or theories explored, well at least not in front of me.

What is happening to Tina and the dignified sister whilst I am in the hospital with this child who is going to be the undignified sister in this story? If I say that initially I am not sure, does that make me a bad mother? Sheila did tell me that she had ‘baby sat’ whilst the dad was visiting us with a swift half thrown in as well. My two helpers came to visit and we laughed about the day, (well you can afterwards), they both admired the baby commenting that she would soon grow. Then of course the two sisters came and held her for a short time Tina declaring ‘let me’ in her loudish way. Some of the nurses took quite an interest in Tina, and you never know may have decided to turn to care for the mentally handicapped (1968) as a career.

My mum arrived to help and visit her new granddaughter, and so another chapter in our lives had begun. We were all happy, and then the small part inside my heart would lurch and I would be back in Germany again in 1963. I did not speak out loud about that time, too painful to contemplate.

One lovely occasion for us was the marriage of my brother in October 1968 and Tina is going to be 10 the day after the wedding. They were not bridesmaids but wore very special clothes and friend Sheila had made them both, undignified sister at 7 months too young, little bags to match their orange pinafore dresses and white blouses. We had a lovely picture of us with the bridal couple but because the undignified sister was crying so much, she was left out of the picture. That I bitterly regret as do I also regret leaving out the baby who has yet to be born (she was crying) from auntie Janet and uncle Mick's wedding picture, and my youngest grandson (he was asleep) from the last family picture before Tina died. So my plea/ advice to the reader is do not leave a child out of a family group does it matter if they are crying or sleeping? As you may also bitterly regret it.

Our lives moved onwards our little girl growing steadily and making herself well known as a very noisy child, she was an undignified sister. The dignified sister is just five and should have started school, but we were moving house and saying goodbye to the camaraderie of the maisonettes. We had been there for two and a half years, but at last with a deposit saved we had found a three bedroom bungalow in North Wootton for £5,250. How times change! The dignified sister would start school there in 1971 after the half term break and Tina would still be at AJ's, on different transport, but she would enjoy meeting a new driver and escort - so onwards and upwards. Our farewells were made but we weren't moving too far away.

Post Scripts

We never heard another domestic from upstairs in fact we never heard any noise at all. Perhaps one of them had gone.

Sheila and I remained firm friends and on Tina's birthdays Sheila would always arrive with some of her family and bring a sausage pie for Tina who preferred savoury to sweet.

Most of the people in our block moved to other areas in North Lynn and even further away. Gloria moving nearer the coast and Sheila into the town.

I did not introduce Marie, coming from Yorkshire she heard my accent and Tina immediately became her close friend. More in the next chapter of Marie and her family.

According to the man who became Tina's best mate, the meatballs were made in America, he knew as he was an engineer installing all the machinery and maintaining it, and having food from there for his pigs. However Gloria insisted that they were made in King's Lynn as she remembered having to put them into the cans. This story could run and run as the best mate disagrees, I cannot waste anymore time on it.

We have sadly left North Lynn.

Outside our maisonette in St. Edmundsbury Road. Tina is ten years old with Rachel and her friend.

Tina with sisters Rachel and Teresa.

Uncle Nigel and Auntie Anne's Wedding Day 26th October 1968. Tina is nine years and two days. Tina and Rachel holding little bags made by Sheila (the lady who does everything) – our good friend.

9

Rill Close

This was another maisonette in a quiet close about four miles from King's Lynn. The dark blue carpet was left for us covering the area of the large L shaped living room. My remembering of the dark blue carpet was because it showed everything that was dropped on to it, and was always in need of vacuuming. Which was why no doubt it was left behind as a gift to us, and why we left it for the elderly couple moving in when we left. There were three bedrooms, a fair sized kitchen and a bathroom, in which the dad painted various circles on the walls, he was artistic and it looked great and helped to take attention from the avocado colour of the bathroom suite.

It was a very different experience moving here, no drama from a 'domestic', in fact we did not hear a sound from upstairs for the two and a half years of living there, but we were quite a noisy family. Actually we seemed to be the centre of the dramas in Rill Close, it was a very genteel area and I am not sure if we ever fitted in. The younger families seemed to have one child each so they were quiet, the older families were out amusing themselves through the daytime and when they came back they were quiet. Then a new family came and they had two boys who were not quiet! This took the pressure off us.

The problem we had living there initially was that the dignified sister's school was quite a walk and Tina's transport arrived after the dignified sister's school started. However it eventually fitted into place, even enabling the undignified sister to start at playgroup. She was definitely not as reserved as her dignified sister and always chose the noisiest children to play with whilst she was there. I remember once that when she and her friend, with whom she was playing at the other child's house, went to the shop at the end of the close and bought themselves a dummy each! Where did they find the money and what did the shop keeper say? Three years old! The mother was frantic when she realised that they had escaped, I could not be angry with her as she was so shocked and very fortunately they had come to no harm.

So after we had recovered from this, we began to have a happy cheerful time in our family, we were all settled into work and play. I had a part time evening job, four nights a week in a factory making fiddly things. I spent the money on driving lessons and eventually passed third time, I was thrilled and thought that life was going to be so much easier for me, the world was starting to be my oyster. But, here comes the crystal ball knowledge I did not have, so I did not know how useful and in what terrible circumstance, the ability to drive was going to be. A life changing necessity for me - but we are not there yet.

Tina is nearly thirteen now and making her own trips to the corner shop with a note for bread or milk and a little something for herself. She was as ever enjoying her life, although I did notice that she did not find as many places to scrounge a biscuit, and I am really sure that she did not wander into anyone's bedroom whilst they were still in bed! Reserved, well brought up people, with no knowledge of disability always had a guarded look when Tina approached, not unkind or hostile but, I think unsure of the right thing to say. Then Tina would ask her CV questions and we would all laugh politely. She did not get much information though, and when I could see that it was a problem for the 'victim' I pretended that we had to be elsewhere. She was settled onto her new bus enjoying the new driver and escort, and it was school Monday to Friday back home for tea-time, and the weekends.

In 1971 there was an upheaval as our currency was going metric. For a short time after arriving back from school there was a programme on the television entitled 'granny gets the point' to help all of us to understand decimalisation. We would sit together and watch how easy it was to change from pounds shillings and pence to pounds and pence, and Tina would lay out all her money to count. Many years later Tina was walking back to our house when suddenly she stops, puts her bag down, takes her purse out of her handbag, opens it and starts to take her money out of the purse and proceeds to throw it into the hedge of our garden where she was spotted by 'best mate' Tony! She said that it was too heavy and she didn't want it, 'what a waste' thought the 'best mate' so it was decided to buy a china pig money box for Tina to put all her change in for the NSPCC. So 'Good job and all' and no more sprinkling of money but... one day Tina had run out of money and broke the pig to take some money out!

One day in Sainsbury's, for some reason Tina and I were in the shop together and Tina was going to pay for her goods. She looked in her purse and on seeing only change tipped the whole amount out on the counter, the coins then rolled onto the floor, leaving the poor assistant to pick out the money that Tina owed. I went over, much to Tina's annoyance, and started to collect some of the money. The poor assistant was even more bewildered until I told her that I was Tina's mum. 'Best mate' Tony did say that this always happened when she was paying for her goods. I don't know how he knew!

Sometimes the balancing act with Tina and her sisters having their individual freedoms, could be tricky but it was all possible. Tina at the age of twelve going on thirteen, was not able to access the friends that she had made at AJ's, as her contemporaries without a disability could do, so it was up to us as a family to provide entertainment outings and visits. We would try to have Wendy from North Lynn and John (he is a new character), around when that was possible. Both of these families could drive so that worked out quite well.

Wendy was the eldest, born in March 1958, then Tina October 1958, and bringing up the rear is John February 1959. John had plenty of girl friends and he alternated between them one after the other, and then caught up with Wendy again. I can't remember Wendy having any other boy friends and Tina was always in love, usually with someone's husband!

John's parents were elderly, routine was their philosophy, and they were very protective of their son. I just had a small issue about John's clothes. Did he have to look like his dad? In beige colours! He had sandy coloured hair and a reddish skin and someone must have said that beige would go with his skin tone. Tina was once invited there for her tea, but when I went to pick her up Vera, John's mum, came to the door wearing a beige cardigan and a worried look.

"Joesssette I was a bit worried y' see she wanted to go to the toilet (and I'm thinking oh god or gosh I hope she didn't make a mess but that wasn't the issue this time) and she dint come down so I said to John we'll have to go see if she's alroight so John and me went upstairs and she was sitting on John's bed y see and I dint know if you'd want her to do that!"

At last a pause for breath. I didn't know what she wanted me to say. Apart from messing up the bed as in ruffling it up did she think Tina may get pregnant? There are always some strange old wives tales going round.

"John did you mind Tina sitting on your bed" I thought that would be safe.

John looked at his mum for an answer,

"Oh no" said mum, "you dint mind did you John?"

And John replied "no Joesssette I dint mind did I mum?"

I reminded Tina to thank Vera for her tea and we drove off waving at the threesome as John and Mum had been joined by dad at the doorway all three still looking worried. That must have 'frit' the life out of Vera and so Tina did not visit on her own again. I don't think Tina was bothered because when I asked if she had had a good time she muttered something like 'boring'.

Wendy would be brought by her mum who would stay for the entire visit and the children, including Tina's siblings, would play with dolls and a pram if the sisters would allow sharing. They did not mind Wendy holding the dolls as she was careful but Tina was rough and the dignified sister particularly did not like her possessions damaged. Tina and Wendy would concentrate on a jigsaw, this was equality as both could find the pieces, but the younger sisters were not so interested so they did their own thing.

It was nice to chat to Hilda, Wendy's mum, she was roughly 20 years older than myself, from Somerset originally and softly spoken. She served in the 2nd world war in an important role, when she met and married Wendy's dad who was from Kings Lynn, and so they returned here after the war. (A foreigner like myself). She then became a full time mum to her 7 children.

The thread that held us together, as with so many of my friends and acquaintances, was our disabled children. We were a part of a club whose members smiled in a knowing, secret way when passing each other on the street or in a shop. We knew that we all shared similar experiences and wishes for the best future possible for our children, realistically knowing that our paths would not be smooth and we would have to be strong - not quite meeting and greeting, but as good as.

This made me realise how alone I was in Germany as I did not know anyone with whom to share this camaraderie. Thinking back now, I realise how bleak my life was, and the baby's death was the final straw. What is the opposite of the icing on the cake? My wretched existence seemed inevitable to me at that time.

Hilda and Wendy particularly liked to come when my Mum and Dad were visiting. Actually mum and dad behaved in our house as if they were in their own, Dad bossing visitors around in his charming way, but they were very popular and went down a bomb with everyone we knew. Mum would just have to clear away the last of the tea cups because she didn't want find them still there when she got up! She was an early riser and used to enjoy her quiet times on her own, before my noisy family were up, and I later did exactly the same!

Another couple of my parent's age were the Barkers from Manchester but now living in King's Lynn, and we became firm friends. Arnold had been the mayor more than once, a thin quietly spoken man, Dot was the absolute opposite, red faced, and plump, and a stalwart worker for the rights of disabled children. They were both ardent socialists so I got on quite well with them, and with the dad being on the 'other side' and Tina joining with him, we had some good debates but everything ended amicably at the end of a session, probably as the dad wanted to go to the pub.

During the school summer holidays with Mungo Gerry on the radio singing 'In the summer time', my auntie used to come down from Leeds to stay for a week, and she would bring at least two of her grand daughters. The children all loved the company and we would all head off to the beach with me driving them in the mini in the days before seat belts, or we would not have fitted all seven in it. As we travelled we all sang, Tina would request songs that no one else knew, so she went solo and I must admit there were a few titters, in the nicest possible way, as to Tina's pronunciations.

All this hilarity in a car returning from a beach trip transported me back to when I was a child and returning from a Sunday school outing with Jean Fletcher who started singing. We were all giggling and tittering, she joined in the giggling as well and had a wonderful ride home being the star of the bus. I remember feeling so pleased that Jean was joining in and laughing and joking, was something preparing me for my future?

As aunty's family grew into young women, the countryside lost its appeal and we began to meet up with them when they came to Butlins at Skegness, where we could get a day pass and take advantage of the funfair and entertainment. Of course Tina was in her element, the friendly atmosphere, the rides, food and a swimming pool. Tina could not swim yet, she was too afraid to go forwards onto her tummy, but she was not afraid of going under so she had a good time with the dignified sister on the slide. She was a bit big for it but no one complained probably because they could see she had 'summat wrong wi 'er! The undignified sister was not comfortable in deeper water and so she just paddled.

One day we went to Caister where auntie Janet had a job in the holiday camp and after her shift we went onto the beach. Uncle Brian (who did not come in the van to the maisonette), auntie Jean and their son must have been staying with us so there was quite a large group of us. It was a nice warm day and we were relaxing, but I have to add being vigilant as to the children's whereabouts. Suddenly I said that I could not see Tina and no one else could either.

"She can't have gone far" said the dad "Let's have a look". So we set off some staying behind to look after the children.

We spoke to various people and asked if they had seen a young girl in a black swimming costume who was 'a bit handicapped', although sympathetic no one had, so after half an hour we decided to call the police as we were really worried by now. I do remember saying to her dad how many more times do you think we will be having to look for

Tina? Eventually the police contacted us (how?) to say that a family had just brought a young girl answering to Tina's description into the police station, wearing only her costume but the family had left her a towel. Evidently they had been walking around with Tina to try and find us at the same time as we were walking around looking for her. She was sitting quietly looking small and apprehensive when we got there, and was overjoyed to see us and the three of us shed a few tears and then all felt better.

"Tina we've been looking everywhere for you!"

She may have replied "don't go on about it."

The police were very kind and explained that the people Tina had chosen to spend her afternoon with had to leave as they were on a bus trip, but were going to ring to see if she had been reunited with her family, we asked to thank them from us. I wonder if this family had filled in their CV!

Yes we did have many more times of Tina searching but none quite as worrying as that.

The dad and uncle Brian would have had plenty to talk about in the pub that night. People in rural pubs always seem to know each other, and 'everyone' either knew, or knew of, Tina so already she was a celebrity in her own right. The dad was still on the committee of the KL society for mentally handicapped children and their families, and they were raising money to build the hydro therapy pool at the school, so it was always handy to be able to sell raffle tickets for the said charity in the pub. That promoted the idea that people with 'summat wrong wi' em' could enjoy the same leisure activities as the general population, and it opened the minds of the pub-goers to a group of people who they may have never realised existed. When she was older Tina accompanied her dad and became an ambassador for Down's syndrome just by being herself, an amusing, interesting, thoughtful person getting on with her life.

Back to Rill Close and the introduction of another of Tina's slaves. Jim was a lecturer at the college, and came to live very temporarily in an upstairs maisonette with his wife Marie, and their four boys. Marie and I actually met when she brought her three year old and her seven month old to the Tufty club and Marie heard my accent and recognised a fellow Yorkshire woman. Once Tina had met Marie it was a match made in heaven, or to be more frank, Tina acquiring a slave.

Tina decided that she liked Irish folk songs and one song in particular which actually had been banned. Tina did not care.

"Marie sing (better not say)"

"No Tina I can't it's banned"

"Don't be daft Marie sing it"

Marie would look around to see if anyone was listening and then would begin to sing quietly,

"The judge said stand up-----

"Can't hear it Marie sing louder"

Tina could be quite tyrannical and insist that the song must be at the correct volume and eventually Marie would comply.

Marie would sometimes come and 'baby sit' for us if the dad could not get one of his students to come…..yes we did go out unaccompanied at times. I would give some instructions regarding Tina's bed time, the younger ones usually already settled beforehand, and so we would leave Marie with our television for the evening, thinking she would welcome a choice of viewing. However Tina would have her own plans, she had a penchant for American shows Dallas and Hawiian five O, the' not to be missed ones', but they were shown at a later time so this did not interfere with Coronation Street which was a great favourite of Marie's and still was with Tina. So they watched it together, then no doubt Marie would bribe Tina with a rendering of 'the banned one' and Marie would be left in peace to eat the cream cake I had bought for her.

This is a picture to show the friendship of these three. Lots of meetings took place at Rill Close in North Wootton where we lived.

10

Woodland Gardens

The dad was a restless character. Was that the forces influence? Perhaps. During his 'swift half' episodes in the pub he picked up the gossip of the area. On one occasion he heard about the development on Woodland Gardens. They were building four bedroom properties and the starting asking price was £10,000!! It is 1972. I was not sure, and didn't immediately agree to a move there, but it was an estate, which is an asset when your children are young, very close to the school for Tina's siblings, they may be able to walk home, and Tina would always have transport to pick her up.

We went to look and were impressed (very). For £10,000 we would have a front door (which was actually at the side) which led into the entrance hall, from where you could access all the downstairs rooms;- a very large kitchen diner with a door into the back garden; a small room for whatever; a very large lounge which ran for the whole length of the front area, excuse the repetition of very large. Oh and I nearly forgot, there was a cloak room in the hall, well it was a toilet and small sink, by the front door….. By the front door! For a family who never closes doors, including toilet doors, it could have tricky moments. Upstairs are four bedrooms, I am not sure over 50 years later where the bathroom and toilet were, but the walls in the bathroom were given the same treatment as in Rill Close i.e. circles. A largish garden at the back, small at the front and a garage at the side with a connecting gate/door from front to back finished the picture. Oh, and the drive was tarmac.

Much larger and smarter than we had ever had. Are we becoming posh?

Let's do it, and we did, after getting a good price for the bungalow of nearly £13,000 pounds.

The children settled into estate life very quickly, as I had predicted, always a child knocking on the door to see if dignified or undignified sister could play out, or there would be a constant procession into the garden to play on the swings. Not as easy for Tina but she either joined in with the other children or visited their parents. The first lady who called Tina by her name as in "Hello Tina" became her best buddy. Tina genuinely loved people, so the more she was brought into contact with all around her, the more she thrived, and of course there were always different biscuits to try! It was a very friendly environment and we became settled and happy.

We arrived here at the beginning of the summer of 1972, dare I hope that fate would start to look favourably on us, did I want a crystal ball to look into - better not - let us stay with this summer of warmth, settlement and joyfulness. And...Tina was going to be a bridesmaid!

Remember little fat Dorothy, (and little thin Arnold her husband) the stalwart worker for the KLS for MHC and their families, well their younger daughter was going to be married to an Irish man in the Roman Catholic church, and the bride-to-be thought it would be a nice experience for Tina being a bridesmaid as she might not get asked again.

Tina's sisters did look lovely in their M and S matching dresses, but Tina, in a pale lemon long dress with other pastel colours vaguely mixed in, topped off with a yellow bonnet, and long hair flowing underneath looked fantastic. I am looking at the photo as I write this, Tina is holding her posy of mixed yellow flowers absolutely correctly, and on her face is a look of composure not often seen I must admit. We were all very proud of her as she had risen to the occasion. But inevitably there was a little hiccup earlier in the day.

We had all bathed, dressed, cleaned teeth, curled hair, tidied the nails of the bridesmaid to be... what did she wear on her feet? Oh yes a pair of slipper type shoes, not for walking, remember this was show time. I had just put my little white suit on that I had bought off the market and a pair of sandals with a higher heel than I usually wear, and shouted down the stairs for someone to make sure Tina was not helping herself to a biscuit as crumbs or sticky would not have worn well on the dress when eventually came back the answer which I always dreaded.

"Don't know where she is."

"Whadyou mean!" Shouted/screamed myself. "Is anybody looking for her! She's got her bridesmaid clothes on"!! As if they had forgotten.

They charged off round the neighbours, the little girls coming up trumps and returning with the prize.

I have a photo of myself stood at the door with my hand on my head, with a little procession of dignified and undignified sisters plus the missing bridesmaid bringing up the rear. The dad must have taken the picture.

"Tinerr" was all I could say. When Tina was found and returned relief was the first emotion, and then irritation hence, the "Tinerr whereve you bin." She wasn't sure but the lady who she had been to visit and show off her outfit came to apologise. She must have heard me shouting.

"I didn't give her a drink or a biscuit, I didn't want her to spill anything onto her dress".

'Thank god for small mercies' I thought.

Doesn't she look lovely," was her parting remark, with me making sure we had all 'been' to the toilet, myself holding up Tina's dress to make sure it was kept in a pristine condition. We then drove off to the church to meet up with the rest of the bridal party, neighbours waving as we did so.

Tina behaved impeccably and basked in the attention and compliments.

I kept the skirt part of the dress as the top quickly became too small for her, and the bonnet, which I came across when I was clearing out the top of the wardrobe. I dare not touch as it looked as if it would crack and break into a thousand pieces.

Time has elapsed and we are well bedded into our lives in WG.

What is Tina doing at school now you may be wondering? Well the perfectly made samplers of various stitches ceased to arrive back home with her, perhaps the message had been received by the head teacher that I did not believe that she could have produced such items. She is in the top class and the teacher Mrs R had decided that Tina should be reading more, hurrah something useful and she was able to pick up the television magazine and recognise programmes which had a special interest to her. Lots of detectives/dramas mostly American, Charlie's Angels, Hawaii Five 0, Columbo the list is endless and Tina was engrossed with her face pressed up to the television at the most exciting moment.

"Sit back Tina you'll ruin your eye sight."

Tina is nearly 16 now and although she was to have a party at the weekend following her birthday I thought she should have an outing on the night. I knew that there was a club (PHAB) for folks with a Physical Handicap and Able Bodied, merging the two together to try and eliminate discrimination was the thinking behind this venture. I always kept my ear to the ground for news of places that would not only be suitable but welcoming as well, I was told that there were some members with a learning disability so I thought why not, and told the dad that I was going to take Tina that night. He wasn't in favour for two reasons; the first Tina might not be welcome and what would I do then? The second, he would be looking after the siblings and would not get out for the swift half. Well, not until we returned.

Tina and I arrived at a place called Crossroads where during the day elderly people were brought in to be cared for. I cannot truthfully say that we were greeted with open arms in fact it was almost as if we had to produce a password.

"You are supposed to let us know that you are coming and no one is allowed under 16 to become a member."

The man on the door was talking to me about Tina, who had wandered into the room.

This was reminding me of when I had sneaked Tina into AJ's after we had been in Yorkshire for a year.

"Well we did not know who to contact so I thought I would bring Tina along to see if she fitted in. She is 16 years old today."

"We haven't got a cake" he replied.

"Tina will have a cake on Sunday with her family and friends, is it all right for her to stay tonight?"

"You will have to stay with her because she isn't a member yet."

I didn't bother to say that I had no intention of leaving her after this hostile welcome.

Well things improved a bit and Tina circled the room telling all she engaged with that it was her birthday and

'am sixteen'!

One nice person decided to sing Happy Birthday.

We were invited to return on the proviso that I would stay with her, and that was the beginning of my support to a club which provided leisure time for folks with a physical disability and then the gradual creeping in of the mentally handicapped 1973. Life was not easy for either group and the more vociferous of the ph folks did not want the mh ones in their club, so the 'marriage' of the two groups eventually had to come to an end, each group going its separate way.

We can safely move on to the summer of 1973 when we were going to go on holiday to Cornwall and the sister of the bride offered us her caravan. Also holidaying at the same time were Marie, Jim and their 4 boys. Marie had done a two week nursing session at Campbells and I think she had spent all her wages on their products, so their car was loaded with boxes of meat balls as well as all their camping gear and clothes. Marie was not an early riser, so Tina would position herself at the tent door (opening) and repeatedly asked Jim,

"Is she up yet".

Jim was very patient and kept saying,

"Not yet Tina" yes a patient man as this question was asked over and over, with myself and the dad trying to persuade Tina to leave the tent opening and play with the sisters, but to no avail as Tina remained at her post until an exclamation of delight -

"At last"!

We knew that Marie had surfaced. This continued for 2 weeks.

The holiday proceeded in this happy vein and when we travelled in cars, Tina would always demand to go with Marie so Jim drove their car with Tina in the front, and us two mums in the back and the dad had the rest of the children with him. Tina was in her element, in the front making comments about the journey and directing Jim to pass the dad, which fortunately he ignored, and then demanding Marie sing 'this is my lovely day'. Tina preferred to hear Marie as she would say,

"She can't sing" gesturing to me.

Marie thought I could, so we took it in turns and Tina had to be satisfied with this arrangement. Ivor Novello tunes as in 'We'll gather Lilacs,'etc were big favourites of Marie's so we sang lustily and then Marie throwing a few Irish ditties into the mix, with Tina repeatedly asking for 'the banned one' but she had to wait until we had arrived at yet another lovely beach. Then the holiday was over, the meatballs had all been consumed, and we set off on our journeys home.

On the way home Tina managed to lock herself in a toilet, and after we had spent quite a long time trying to direct her to push/pull on the handle, the dignified sister had to scrape underneath the door to release her.

"Don't lock the door again Tina" we all said to her.

"No I won't" she said.

I thought, 'until the next time.'

Tina learnt to swim when she was 19 years old. We were on holiday in Bled which was in the former Yugoslavia. A lady staying in the same hotel, who was a swimming instructor, walked up and down the pool with Tina holding around her waist and kicking her legs. This put Tina into the correct swimming position and within quite a short time she gradually let go of the lady and she was off! Hooray. We clapped and cheered. It was wonderful to see her becoming more and more confident and so that was the beginning of many many happy years of swimming, and boasting about it. We were so grateful to that lady.

Well after a few weeks back home it was quite nice to find out that I was pregnant again! In late 1973 a test called an amniocentesis for Down's syndrome was available, taking a sample of amniotic fluid surrounding the baby, and studying the chromosome count on trisomy 21? If there is an extra cell parents can be given the option of a termination and I naively thought it would be nice to know that everything was 'alright', an abortion was not in my mind at all. The doctor agreed to this as I did have a child with Down's. I correctly used the word naively, because I did not understand that there was a risk of the fluid leaking and when I got home from this procedure and sat in a chair, then shall I say 'ruptured membranes', and all females who have given birth will understand, well perhaps both genders would.

The dad just said,

"Well get up then" as I was sat on a good chair.

Upshot! I was taken into hospital for my condition to be monitored. The outpourings became less and the pregnancy continued. After 9ish weeks of waiting for the result I was told that the sample was blurred, inconclusive and the doctor asked if he should do it again, a firm *'no' was my answer.*

A seven and a half pound baby girl arrived the day after the due date, (the largest of my children again with a normal diagnosis). It was so nice to have a child with a decent birth weight and all the family were thrilled with her. My friend Dot was looking after the baby's siblings and after popping in to see us contacted my parents to say,

"Oh Irene your new granddaughter has a tiny nose, a rosebud mouth, beautiful blue eyes and rosy cheeks."

This was the child who Tina first showed off her talent of making a popping noise with her finger inside her hollow cheek and the baby sister's eyes would open widely and then blink as if to say 'What is my sister doing!' Apart from my mum, from whom she had learnt this talent, Tina was the only one who could do it so it became her party piece, and every baby or young child with whom Tina came into contact, was given this treatment.

Let us move forward and the baby sister is about 12 months old and nearly walking, and Tina was 17 and fast approaching the time when she would be leaving A.J. school, and we were going to be visited by an assessor. He was a doctor from another area, without any pre conceptions of her ability or suitability to decide the next move. Tina had to have the day off from school which she wasn't that keen on, but

"Tina how can he assess you if you are not here?"

"Oh alright fusspot what about ma transport?"

"I told the driver yesterday when you came back."

Tina had to accept that she would have to remain with myself and the baby sister.

The visiting doctor arrived just after baby sister had been put into her cot for her morning nap. Tina had been pre-warned as to not go off on a tangent, i.e. do not ask him to fill in a cv.

"How many sisters and brothers do you have?"

I was anxious, as I was not sure if she was going to mention the lost baby and what to say if she did, I couldn't have coped with the explanation, but Tina concentrated on her sisters and said that baby sister was 'in her cot sleeping'

We then discussed hobbies, wrestling had become one of Tina's favourites with Big Daddy and Giant Haystacks in particular, the doctor made a polite comment when Tina asked him if he liked watching wrestling on the television.

"I don't think I have ever managed to see that Tina".

"You should" she replied.

Then onto Crossroads and Coronation St - the doctor hadn't seen them either. I could see that Tina was feeling sorry for him - then we discussed what Tina could do for herself in personal care (most things), what she could do to help in the home (as little as she could get away with).

"Can she go to the shop by herself?"

"Course I can," was Tina's immediate reply.

I just added, "with a note".

I could see that Tina was enjoying it all and I was a little worried that the doctor may be running out of time, and we were now coming to where Tina would be moving on to when she left AJ's.

I am sure it was a done deal that she would go to the Adult Training Centre which would include some time at the college to carry on with reading and money management, there was the opportunity for cooking, gardening, painting and concreting at the ATC, and some PE thrown in. Just then I heard a cry from upstairs and excused myself, leaving the doctor in Tina's clutches. I heard Tina asking did he want another coffee or biscuit and was slightly relieved when he replied "no thank you Tina" to both. I was a longer time upstairs as baby sister needed changing as she had done a poo. Tina guessed this and said when we came down,

"What've you done you stinker?"

Baby sister broke into loud cries so Tina did her famous pops and all became well again.

We were coming to the end of the interview, and the doctor asked Tina if she had any questions to ask him?

Tina wriggled around a bit on her seat which always meant that she had something to say but you were never sure what it was going to be.

"Yes I have" she said.

"Oh what is it Tina?"

More wriggling...."Are you married?" Well I wasn't surprised as she had contained herself as to asking for his cv and he did ask.

"Erm --- Yes I am" finally came out.

And Tina was for once satisfied with this short answer and so we said our goodbyes baby cheering up after he had gone and Tina a bit sheepishly saying,

"Was that alright mum?"

"Yes Tina 'course it was. And isn't that great that you are going to the ATC and college."

Tina's relationship with dignified sister could be really stretched at times e.g. the dignified sister had been given a long playing record by the Drifters for her birthday, by a boy she had a crush on, and Tina immediately pounced on it and thought she could take it to the centre the next day.

"No Tina you can't, dignified sister has just had that given as a present. Ask her to play it for you here."

There was silence from Tina which I should have realised was ominous, no complaining of me being a fuss pot or trying to persuade her sister. The next day after Tina had left I thought I should look to see if the record was still in the box in the dignified sister's bedroom, I could not see it anywhere, could she have taken it with her to school - 'I doubt it' which was a phrase Tina used when she became much older, and it fits nicely in here. I looked in Tina's bedroom. No sign.

It was a long day until they arrived back. The dignified sister returned earlier but I dare not ask her if she had taken it that morning, I would have to wait for Tina! She arrived back with her large bag and I waited until dignified sister was not around and then I broached the subject.

"Tina did you take dignified sister's new record to the centre today?"

"What record?" she was stalling.

"You know Tina her new Drifters one"

"Oh that, it's in ma bag."

"Get it out and let me look"

"Alright fuss pot".

Tina was playing the casual criminal and bluffing her way through.

I did not bother to say that I had thought all day what if someone had taken a bite out of it. It would not have been the first time that items had come back, 'not intact', shall I say.

The box looks fine I thought, and then I proceeded to take off the paper slip which was covering the first record I was to examine. That was fine, so far so good, but then the next one had a missing edge as in a bite mark. Am I a clairvoyant or just a worst scenario realist? This news had to be broken to the dignified sister who actually was looking for her records and shouting down the stairs had I seen it. Has undignified sister had it,

"No I don't want that blooming old record," she had replied and then

"Has Tina taken it to the centre Oh mum has she damaged it?

What could be said to that?

"Keep calm ds" says Tina in a not very confident voice.

"Where is it?" .....

Tina had to hand over the ruined record that only 24 hours ago was a much loved present. Well there was wailing and sobbing from dignified sister, and even undignified sister and baby sister were joining in the many comments that were being hurled at Tina, and myself as, according to all my family, I should have checked Tina's bag before she left that morning. Well when under stress blame the mum! We decided that the record could be played by putting the needle just over where the abomination had taken place. Eventually the drama became a history, we all learned to laugh about it and whenever 'boardwalk' was played we began to smile at the memory. Mind you Tina was quite chastened after this and minded her p's and q's for the next few days at least.

Tina has always been an excellent time keeper and if I was involved with baby or perhaps an older sis then she would make sure she was ready for the mini bus with me shouting as to had she got everything in her bag.

"Course I 'ave bye"

And she would be gone, again with me shouting for someone to wave her off. (In my family if someone left the house the ones remaining would go into 'the room', which was at the front of the house, and wave until the person was out of sight. I thought every family did that.)

The downstairs room in Woodland Gardens near to the front door, housed a cabinet containing amongst other things, a bottle of Martini, and while I was in there looking for whatever, I happened to put my hand on the cabinet shelf and discovered it to be sticky. I cannot bear sticky! On further investigation I happened to notice (like a detective), that the martini bottle top was not secure and it did not have much left in it..... ALSO THERE WAS A STICKY GLASS. 'Tinerrr' was all I could think.

On her return and after further questioning it transpired that she had been having a glass of martini whilst waiting for the mini bus! What would have happened when she had finished the bottle, and could the escort smell alcohol in the van? Nobody had said anything!

"Tinerrr don't do that again there are times and places to have a small drink and not before you go to school!"

"Alright fusspot."

Thinking about it, we had never spoken about allowances for Tina, she was not included in the family allowance system as she would proudly say,

"I'm the oldest y'know."

But should she have been having an allowance now that she is approaching 18 but not able to work or run her own affairs or should it have been for us to support her? The dad found out there should be, during one of his swift half sessions from W's dad, as she was older than Tina, who said that parents had to discover this for themselves. So Tina—we—was/were, entitled to an attendance allowance. How many parents would have had to struggle financially before this knowledge began to filter out to them? It was an issue that was discussed at the KLSforMHC's next meeting, and eventually all social workers had to relay this information to the families to whom they had a responsibility.

Something jolly to talk about, Tina will soon be 18 and she will be having a very frivolous party.

This is where the dad comes into his own. The fish and chip shop whose lease he had taken over 3 years ago was obviously doing well so he engaged a Country and Western singer, Tina's favourite genre, to perform with her group at the party. Tina had often been with him when this singer came to Kings Lynn and so she was over the moon when she knew Patsy P was coming. She would have been even further over the moon if it had been Dolly Parton but even the fish and chip shop takings could not have reached that far. Tina wore a lovely chiffon type lemon and white dress (not the bridesmaid dress), she did look very pretty and she and every one had a great time. I still have the long playing record which Patsy gave to Tina with all the band's signatures written on it.

Very sadly now we are coming to….how do you say for the second time that your world, your life is going to become unbearable? Remember the little undignified sister? Please don't forget her. She is 9 years old now and has always been a spiky child. I found a picture of her yesterday looking quite serene, smiling quietly and the huge gap in between her two front teeth was showing, she always tried to hide it when photographs were being taken. One of the songs of the time was 'Brown Girl in the Ring' which in my head became her song. In the photo she is wearing an orange top but everything else is brown, hair, eyes, skirt, socks and shoes. What was happening to her now this spiky child? I didn't know but everything was becoming more extreme...anger and then tiredness fought with each other to take control.

We went to the doctors, she was a no nonsense doctor who as the saying says she 'did not suffer fools or time wasters gladly.' She agreed with me the undignified sister would need to have some tests, she was sent first to the local hospital and then on to Addenbrookes, a highly regarded hospital in 1977. I have never been there again.

Numerous tests later we were told that there was a tumour in her brain and the tests were to show where it was before an operation could take place. The CAT scan showed some, but not all the information.

Can you imagine the upheaval in our household. The depths to which we were to be plummeted. We were all in this together, all in our different ways but some semblance of life had to go on. The baby sister was only two, the poor dignified sister who was thirteen had the hardest time as she understood the most, the dad tried to carry on at the college and at the fish and chip shop and pretend that it would be alright. What is Tina doing you may ask was she keeping calm and carrying on, was she missing me, her mum and the spiky undignified sister? Of course she was, but I didn't really know the extent of this with any of my other children because my place in my head and my heart was with this gravely ill little girl. My mum came down and picked up the pieces with help from neighbours, friends and family. Very sad for mum as she was still trying to function after my dad's fairly sudden and untimely death at the age of sixty four from a heart attack or myocardial infarction to give the proper title.

The day the prognosis was given to the dad and myself, it wasn't a Sunday possibly Friday as some bad news is better before the weekend. Better for whom? Certainly not us but surgeons have to be blunt and the truth had to be told. No operation, too dangerous a place and he was going to give this child over to a doctor who would decide how much radio and chemotherapy she could have.

I suddenly thought, 'No. I have had my turn it should be someone else I can't do that again and I kept screaming 'it's not my turn I've been through this agony before I can't do that again.' The doctor and his assistant just waited and looked down at the table which was separating us, the broken hearted parents, the dad was also beginning to cry, for the little girl that he was so frustrated he could not help.

Eventually I calmed down a bit. You cannot scream for the rest of your life and there was a child to be supported and I knew I would jolly well have to get on with it. When I had calmed down enough I went back to the ward where she was sleeping peacefully. I felt cheated, cheated because I wanted to see her head covered in a huge bandage like in the films when you know something bad has happened but everything will be alright now because the thing in the head has gone and the bandage is the proof of that. And there will be a happy ending. But that was a film and this was the reality of the situation. No operation.... the radiotherapy would begin soon.

What happens when a doctor goes home after this sharing of information which has compressed and tightened and shrivelled your heart your brain and lungs but had the opposite effect on your bowel and bladder? Does he forget when he is in his car driving home, when he greets his family when he arrives, when perhaps his wife might ask about his day, would he say that he had distraught parents of little girl to impart a death sentence to, because that is what it was. Perhaps to him it was an ordinary day.

A Dr W (cancer specialist) came to see us, and explained what was going to happen. For all the time he was in charge and monitoring the treatments, I clung on to him like one of the limpets in Cornwall. That happy carefree time felt like a million years ago. My time was divided into being at the hospital, going back at night to a good friend's house in

Cambridge then occasionally back to Woodland Gardens to spend a night with the family. Wasn't it a good thing (A1 would have said a blessing) that I had learned to drive?

Somehow living in the hospital which I nearly was, and then leaving at the end of the day, it was a shock to see the rest of the world just getting on with their lives, driving, walking, outside a school, shopping, laughing, talking…..all this normal activity makes you feel cut off, abandoned by a world to which you have ceased to belong.

Charlie and the Chocolate Factory was the book I read to Teresa, I think she must be an individual now in her own right and be referred to with her own name. She was too tired to read herself and she enjoyed me reading to her. When she slept I sometimes laid my head next to her on the pillow. This must have been reported on because I was told by an official that someone would come and read to her and I could go off and do something. 'Like what?' Tina would have said. I thanked her quite politely but said that I wanted to stay and read to her. She didn't seem too happy with that answer but she left me alone. She might have been thinking of me in this predicament or the tidiness of the ward. Then sometimes we would walk a little way around the hospital and then back to the neurology ward, she was never in the children's ward I am not sure why.

Then a nice little break…..she was allowed home and leaving the hospital behind somehow in my muddled head it was as if we were leaving the cancer behind. A comical thing on the way home she removed the wig she was wearing and waved it at the driver of the car behind which was travelling too close to us on a bendy road! She was regaining her spirit!

Sadly it did not last for long. Radium treatment does not last forever against the bullish behaviour of an aggressive cancer and so after chemotherapy which made her whole body bloated which distressed her greatly as being a thin gangly child she could not bear to see herself turning into something that was becoming painful for all of us to see. One day Tina's friend Marie (the banned song singer) came to visit us before going back to Harrogate (they had left the K L college behind at this time 1978) and there was just Teresa and I in, as her siblings had gone for the swift half, and she was helping to cook the dinner.

We chatted for a while and then on saying our goodbyes I could see that Marie was looking quite tearful after she had told me that I was doing a wonderful job and I thought, 'I am?' this is my child and what else would a parent do and I thought 'please don't cry now as this is being a nice day for us.'

And she did not cry in front of us.

Many many years later I had escorted my grandson to messy church, where I saw a child with his dad who, I had been told by the dignified sister, was suffering from a brain tumour.

The dad was smiling happily and the child was joining in as best he could, and I just wanted to cry as I do now remembering this and thinking back to Marie and her thoughts for me and possibly what I was going through. And on that afternoon I knew why she did not cry in front of me and why I did not cry in front of this dad. You have to put your feelings to one side and the last thing that this dad would want was a woman grieving for him when they were having a good time. As my little girl and I were 40 odd years ago.

The day before she died, Tina and the dignified sister were taken by a friend to Grandma's and the baby sister was taken by her uncle to stay at their house. Should they have stayed with us? All these years later and I still wonder if it was the right thing to do.

When I rang grandma she was waiting for this news and we talked for a little while and after saying I would ring back, the last thing I heard was the dignified sister screaming.

'I'll look after them' said my mum.

This was a time when I envied my mum's religious belief. She knew exactly where Teresa was now while I was left with another huge package of grief that would remain with me forever.

One day I heard the baby sister asking uncle A where Teresa was now, and he had her dressed as an angel sitting perhaps not at God's right hand but near enough. I am not sure what she would have thought of that, but it made baby sister happy.

Teresa's death was in August and at the requiem mass Marie, Jim and Sheila, who were all staunch Roman Catholics took communion in an Anglian church. I thought they were with us in our grief and that was more important than religious dogma.

There was no service available for bereaved siblings. We all had to cope with our grief in our own way, I think it is more advanced now.

Tina's grief would come out in the next chapter.

'There is still no improvement in the life expectancy of children with a brain tumour within the last 40 years'... I heard this statement on the Today programme a few months ago. It is the 2nd most common cancer in children. Leukaemia is the 1st. Surely, surely in all this time could there not have been a small breakthrough?

I used to pass the Oncology unit on my walk from the car park to the door of Addenbrookes and again I would think is there no one in there who could give hope to the grieving families, and more importantly to the children suffering?

At Chrissie and Brendan's Wedding, Tina is now fourteen and this is the first time she is a bridesmaid, the other bridesmaid is Chrissie's niece.

Tina is on holiday in Tintagel in 1972 with her sisters. She is very confidently holding her arm out with a bird perched on it.

Tina aged 15 with her baby sister Louise or W'lice – Tina's name for her.

Tina is in a series of photos on how to strangle your little sister.

11

Serenata

After Teresa's death our time at Woodland gardens also died. It was too uncomfortable, for example every time you set the table for a meal then a place where she used to sit has to be left out. Do you set it and leave it empty? No far too poignant. Do you move all the places to try and create a new theme? No. you just shuffle around. Then the washing. Where is her pile of clothes to be washed? It is now non existent. These are the incidental things which occur as the dismal days follow dismal days. There is no shouting and debating and saying that 'it isn't fair,' no moaning about the teacher who (inTeresa's words) said that the dignified sister was letting her down, no dark eyes twinkling and spreading herself across the fire place eating tangerines....So, impossible to live there surrounded by our memories and to try and save a marriage that was fast dying, we were once again on the move.

Not too far away, possibly 2 miles, baby sister, who had already spent her first term in one school, was moved to another but she did soon settle. The dignified sister, on returning to her secondary school in September (and remember she was only 13 years old) said that nobody, spoke to her about the death of her sister and she didn't know what to say to anyone. One day when I was clearing out a cupboard I found an English exercise book belonging to her, one essay was entitled My Summer Holiday, she wrote a little about her sister's death and got a B plus! I think giving a child a B plus for trying to describe her feelings on losing her sister, with no follow up from the staff, was totally inadequate. Why didn't I say something? I was wrapped up in my own misery.

So different now, there is a wonderful organisation called Nelson's Journey which gives support to children who have lost very close members of their families, this organisation is so important to a bereaved family.

I have not even described this house, well it had a very large lounge and entrance from the front door and the steps to the upstairs led from this opposite the front door. The back door was from a side passage and led into the kitchen which was in a dark area and there were three bedrooms upstairs. Can you sense that my heart was not in this move as it was probably done too quickly? How are you to know what is the best and for whom? May be best for the dad, as the pub he frequented was opposite, but I think the old house was sold too cheaply at the beginning of the 1980's at £35,000. That sounds too cheap add a bit more on!

And Tina what about her, was she managing this move? There was a slightly different bus at a different stop and lots of new people to meet. There was also a pub at the end of the road which she visited either with or without her dad. Her day time activities were the same, she was well settled into the environment of the ATC, or Adult Training Centre, if you have forgotten the abbreviation, and had found another best buddy Mandy, a young girl with cerebral palsy, who lived at Blackborough End. Thank God I could drive as Tina was often invited there and her ability on the buses did not stretch to changing half way, so I would drop her off in the morning come home and do the reverse in the late afternoon. I just thought it was lovely that she could choose her own friends and have some time with Mandy and her mum, however after a few months of this friendship Mandy's family moved back to London, but Tina survived this separation in her own way, with a bounce, and it was all adding to the rich pattern of Tina's life.

My heart was elsewhere during this time, but Tina continued to provide alarms and excursions including an adventure on her bicycle. She had managed very well when younger with a two wheeler bike with stabilisers, but Tina was now 21-ish and it was not appropriate. She tried an adult trike but couldn't steer it very well and so just had a two wheeler that she could get on and off quite easily, but I was not comfortable with Tina riding on the road. School children at the age of 10 or 11 have to pass a cycling proficiency test before they are allowed on the road but what about

Tina and others with a disability, perhaps their parents were sensible, safety conscious, over protective or just think that we were downright stupid or becoming too gung ho?

Maybe people said 'Tina wants to ride a bike on a road to get to the pub?! What is her mother thinking about?'

Yes what indeed was her mother thinking about? Better leave the dad out of it as he was becoming more 'alcohol dependent to be polite' and not responsible for some of his own behaviour, never mind Tina's bicycle jaunts.

I had a phone call early one Saturday afternoon.

"Josette I have just seen Tina riding her bike on the wrong side of the road."

I can't remember who that was but on charging off to look for Tina, I saw her turning into our little close, and looking rather startled to see me.

"Tina I have just had a phone call to tell me you were riding on the wrong side of the road."

"Who was it?" said Tina in a rather irritated way as she did not like to be spied upon.

"It doesn't matter who it was but you were on the wrong side of the road. You might have been knocked down."

"I wouldn't" said Tina in her gung ho style.

She did look very flushed and didn't make a fuss about coming in, and the next minute she was fast asleep on the settee, and then the next day she was covered in chicken pox spots! Caught most likely from her baby sister who was just recovering from said disease. Well that put the cycling to an end and the bicycle was discreetly put to the back of the garage.

I had to break the news to Tina that she would have to stay at home for a little while as she would not be able to go to the centre whilst she was still contagious.

"How long" She demanded to know.

Well baby sister could not go back to school until the spots had a scab on... or come off.

"That's stupid that is."

"Well not really Tina because there are some vulnerable people at the ATC and you would not be allowed to go and pass the infection on. And anyway you will be able to watch your favourites on the tv in the afternoon."

"Like what."

"Well Charlie's Angels or Columbo or Cell Block H," (or was that just on at night, I'm not sure, not being a fan of daytime tv.)

Tina cheered up after that information but I still felt that she thought she was doing me a favour. I actually might have to give up a shift or two at the glass works factory, just a temporary job during school time showing visitors around, but it was good for me although the money was poor.

"Oh alright then I'll stop."

I did not dare to tell neither Wendy's nor John's mum of the bike incident but I had to say about the chickenpox as they were all at the ATC together. Wendy's mum was quite philosophical with Wendy having older siblings but poor Vera, John's mum whisked him off to the doctors just to make sure.

'About what' Tina would have said.

After Teresa had died the dad, apart from finding solace in alcohol, also turned to the church for support. The priest at the seaside church was a friend of a friend of the dads who also went to this church and then to the conservative club afterwards. What would you call it...a farce? To confess your sins but then go into the club to drink with renewed vigour, I may be biased but I could not see what was to be gained. But we are all different and coping with sorrows as cruel as ours, we all progressed or regressed in our different ways, there is no universal formula for this, you just have to stumble through it all.

On one Sunday Tina was adamant that she did not want to come with us to church. So with the vegetables prepared, the chicken in the oven and strict instructions to leave the oven alone, we would be back within the 2 hours that we could safely leave Tina. I was the driver so I stipulated that we would not go to the conservative club afterwards.

Well we went and came back, the dad sulking because I had stuck to my decision to not go into the conservative club.... the swift half would have lengthened and I was not prepared to compromise. We got out of the car and I was surprised not to see Tina bounce out to meet us. Beginnings of worry! These were compounded as we got near to the back door there was a definite smell of burning! We all rushed in and there was Tina stood by the cooker looking at the pans of vegetables boiling and bubbling, the burning smell coming from the peas in a small pan. Under stress mixed with relief because Tina did seem alright, why do people say such obvious things, it was definitely a 'Tinerrr' moment but why ask her what she had done? I could see what she had done, put all the veg on to cook, and I glimpsed Yorkshire puddings in the oven either under or over the chicken, she had cooked the dinner! She did look very tearful as we were analysing the whole situation, and to be fair only the peas had been ruined.

"I never touched the chicken" she said and burst into tears. The dad took her to the pub for the swift half whilst the rest of us cleared up. The dinner went down quite well as we had all cheered up, but we did say Tina don't do that again you could have been badly burnt.

"No I won't" she said.

For once I didn't think she would. I did not tell neither Hilda nor Vera about this.

From then on it has been a family tradition to talk or not to talk about burnt peas in front of Tina, unless she brings up the subject, as in

"Mum, can you remember"

And I or whoever will reply in Tina's voice

"Do you 'ave to".

Then there was Tina and her bedroom. In the bedroom Tina had her bed of course, and on the opposite wall was a bed settee which dignified sister had used before her new bedroom was finished off , and Grandma also either used this or Tina's bed when she came to visit.

Tina came into the kitchen, usually it would be to see how the tea was progressing, but not this time.

"Mum, want to move ma bed."

"What do you mean Tina?" She had said it quite clearly probably I was playing for time. "Where do you want it moved to?"

"Other side where the ssssettee is."*

"I can't help you do that Tina you'll have to wait for your dad to come back. That will be a difficult job."

And indeed it would as there was only a small amount of space between the bed and the end wall and the same with the settee. I could see that Tina was not happy to put her plan on hold until her dad came back and he might tell her she would have to wait until he had more time. She disappeared after telling me she would,

"Do it maself."

I just carried on with the tea preparations, and to be honest I could hear some minor movement from her room and was expecting at any time soon the call of,

"Mum come 'ere am stuck". The call never came and then suddenly Tina appeared in the kitchen,

"Come on then comeanlook."

She was a little breathless and was looking at her hands and making phewing sort of noises.

I went up the stairs wondering as to just what I was going to be greeted with.

"Close yor eyes" was a command Tina used when she was about to show off something i.e. cooking from the college or a tidy sink area.

I did as I was bid and when I was commanded to open them it was with a little bit of trepidation.

Why did I worry. The bed and the settee had, abracadabra, changed places. I looked at the walls no scuff marks, then I proceeded to grill Tina.

---

* Tina was developing a stutter which in this piece manifested itself in the s's, and I thought she should see a speech therapist. I must have spoken to someone at the ATC but she was not regarded as a child anymore so there was no such service. The year could be 1982. Making Tina 24.

"Who's helped you to do this Tina?"

"No one, did it maself"

I was, as the comedian Les Dawson once said, something like my 'ghast had been flabbered'. I shouted out to dignified sister who was revising/snoozing in her bedroom had she helped, but manual labour was not in this sisters' vocabulary and so no was the answer, and just then the dad came in.

"Can you come and see what Tina has done I cannot believe she has done this by herself."

He agreed and then started thinking of people who might have come in to help, but in the end we just had to marvel at the way she must have lifted one bed onto the other and pulled two beds! She must have dragged one some of the way first and then tossed the other over.....? Tina did try to explain and demonstrate, without actually lifting anything, and we had to accept that some sort of a miracle had taken place. It does say something of Tina's character to think that when the odds are stacked against her reaching a goal, which on that day was the repositioning of two large pieces of furniture, she would not accept defeat.

Or did Tina have a guardian angel who on that afternoon noted her problem and came to her assistance, who knows? It might have been the same guardian angel who protected her from the burnt peas episode.

"Tina don't try and move the wardrobe will you".

"Corse I won't" she said.

The story has run and run and I am still thinking of the guardian angel.

One more very sad incident, which needs to be told, and then we must leave this house.

The dignified sister went to dancing classes in the town, I would take her and a friend in, and the other mum or dad would do the return trip. It would take less than 30 minutes for me to drop them off and return. Tina stayed at home because it was East Enders time and it was always a must watch soap. Just baby sister and I went.

On returning and going into the house there were sounds of loud sobbing, which at first I thought was the programme. I wish it had been but it was Tina. She was sitting on the settee with Teresa's last school photograph and was just sobbing and saying she wanted her sister and why did she have to die? I had no answer and we just sat there with our arms around each other until we had both calmed down. I asked if she would like me to put the photo in a drawer and she said,

"Good idea mum, I won't do that again."

I said that it wouldn't matter if she did, because we are all missing her and we all want to have our own moments. And then I thought where is the baby sister, what has she been doing all this time? She had just gone to sit in the kitchen on her own and she was no more than six years old.

Well we all sat together in the lounge before baby sister went to bed and Tina was calm and watching her next programme when dignified sister came back, and it was a few days before she noticed that the photo was missing. We all deferred to Tina's wish to keep the photo in the drawer. Please don't judge us on that, we are all stumbling along.

The organisation, Mencap, used to have a picture of a child who was mentally handicapped who was looking downwards on their correspondence with a sad expression. The figure reminded me of Jean Fletcher - please don't forget her. When the term 'mentally handicapped' became obsolete being replaced by 'Learning Disability' the little figure was not shown anymore, actually it was banned. I suppose what the organisation wanted was a more positive image and not one to create the impression of one who is incapable. The problem to me was that for some people their perception of the mentally disabled was a sweet natured child who would remain unaffected of anything that was happening around them, absolutely not true of Tina who, although it was painful for me to remember the night when she was heartbroken because she had lost her sister, proved how she was as affected as all of us over her death.

Shall we finish Serenata on a less difficult note? Tina had many bags of all shapes and sizes, but on this particular day none would take the item she needed to take, I think it was a folder so she would have been going to the college. All her bags had been tried and discarded and after hearing from me that I did not have one large enough for the folder and turning down the offer of a carrier bag, she, unbeknown to anyone, had gone into her dignified sister's inner sanctum (bedroom), and then into her wardrobe where her bags were kept, in a pristine condition, to see if there was one large enough for the said folder, at least this was my supposition of the events.

I was on the phone speaking to my friend Gloria, when dignified sister came home, went upstairs and I heard her asking Tina what was she doing! There is a very coarse expression of something hitting a fan and that is what was happening in the bedroom. Gloria asked what all the noise was about and I said that dignified sister must have caught Tina raiding her bags! We quickly said our goodbyes and I rushed upstairs to hear dignified sister still screaming to Tina 'look what you've done to my bags' and Tina asking her to calm down. The contents of the main bag had been discarded, Tina's file was half in but would not have fitted, and she was trying to pick up all the discarded stuff, and shove it somewhere else like under the bed. I thought it will be my fault again and it nearly was.

"Mum why did you let Tina near my bags".

"I didn't know she was in your room I was on the phone".

"Well that's typical,"

What was? "Can I help you sort it out".

"No" she squawked "Just take Tina out and leave me alone."

So Tina and I went quietly out and made a cup of tea and after a while dignified sister came down, still fuming but quietly this time.

"Sorry ds" said Tina and she started to cry.

Dignified sister also started to cry and say that she was sorry that she had lost her temper.

"S'alright" said Tina.

I think she must have taken the folder in a carrier bag, and I think that dignified sister must be Rachel, her given name from now on. Or Rach for short.

Tina is looking rather bemused at her 21st birthday party. Someone had made a lovely cake for her. It was club night so everyone joined in She did have a wonderful 18th party but the photographs have vanished.

Tina is on a cookery course, lovely food comes home.

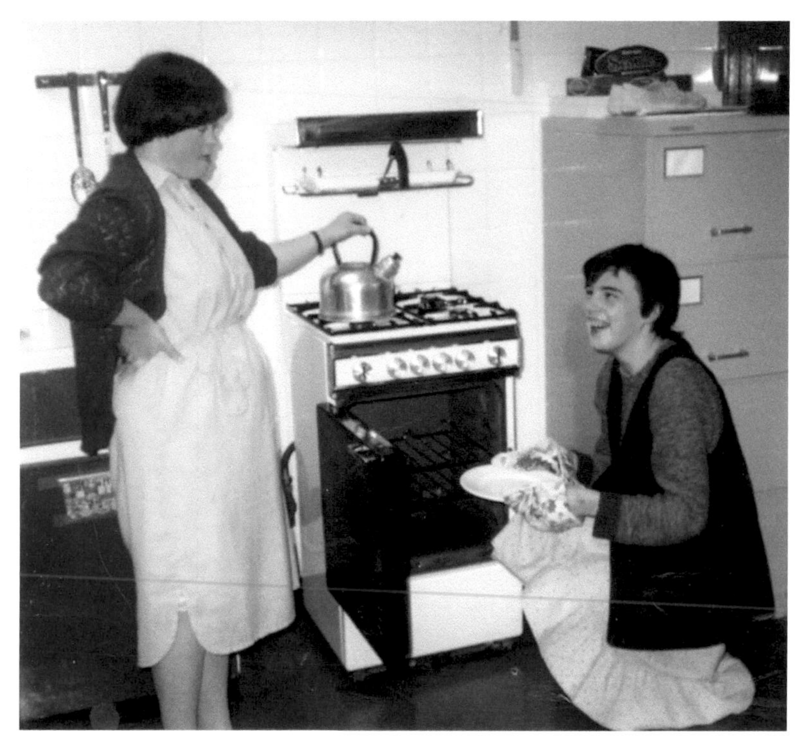

Tina is on the same cookery course with Rosie.

Tina and Karl met when they were on the pilgrimage to Lourdes. They were celebrating Rachel's 18th birthday at the party.

Tina is keeping an eye on Edward and managing to hold at least one leg of her trousers. What had Ed seen?

Tina with sleepy Claire and 'wanting to escape' Will. This was after swimming 50 lengths.

Tina babysitting William in 2006

Babysitting in late Spring 2007 – and now Tony has joined in.

Now Tony is teasing Tina. We are at Fountain Abbey near Harrogate, Yorkshire.

Tina is having a reward, 'Thank you Marie'.

12

Queen's Avenue to Pansy Villa

This little Edwardian house, in what some may have regarded on the wrong side of the tracks, was for me a bolt hole from an impossible situation. The divorce between the dad and myself had gone through but because our house had not been sold, we had to remain connected for another 18 months. 18 months why? Money that was why. No house sale, no money to move on. Never mind me, I have digressed, and it is more important for Tina and her sisters to be thought about.

Tina was still at the ATC and college, and not seeming to be affected, saying that it is a very shallow explanation and usually I would be able to think more deeply into what was going on in Tina's head, my only excuse is that my own thoughts were getting in the way. Rachel was in the middle of her A levels, she had a boyfriend, and she had enjoyed her 18th birthday party which was at the end of 1982, not quite so glamorous as Tina's 18th, but she wasn't such a show off as her sister! Tina also enjoyed her sister's party as her erstwhile boyfriend from the Lourdes trip, Karl, came as well. Tina wore a black and orange fine striped dress in a straightish style with a gold belt tights and high-ish heeled sandals, and the picture in her life book shows it fitted her perfectly. I also think she was in one of her thinner phases possibly all the badminton she had been playing!!

Tina loved a disco especially the twist and she was brilliant at it so much more flexible than the rest of us. Boyfriend Karl seemed to enjoy watching and I was keeping an eye on Mr. K in case he did a runner and try to go home on his own and not wait for his dad! The baby sister who is now nine years old, also enjoyed the whole affair. There is a picture of us all looking very happy, which made it even sadder, knowing the outcome.

Well Serenata was finally sold and I was able from my share to buy Pansy Villa for £24,000 which had been done up stylishly by the previous occupant, it had three bedrooms, two bathrooms, one downstairs with bath and bidet, an en suite in one bedroom and a small kitchen and through lounge finished it off. We lived there for three years and it sold for £39,000, property was on the up, but we are not there yet- except to say that the baby sister who was 12 years old now, was out of her comfort zone and spent most of her time in the South Wootton area where her dad was still living with his girlfriend/partner. I wasn't happy but parents who divorce have to give children a choice whether you think it is right or not.

Tina was able to carry on with all her activities, one of which was the badminton club that was suitable for all disabled people held at the college, and Tina and Wendy always played against each other and from where the spectators were sitting, you could hear a running commentary as in:-

"Come on Tina Swann pick it up." (The shuttlecock).

"Hang on Wendy Nobbs"

Tina would walk in a languid way to pick up the you know what, bend over at the same time lifting her leg high behind her. I can't remember if she ever over balanced. She would then refer to her watch as she picked up the said shuttlecock.

"Tinerrr come on slow coach"

"Oy Nobbie don't say that"

"Tina don't say that my name's Wendy Nobbs. I'll call you Swannee."

"No a can't stand that call me Tina, Nobby"

I banged on the glass, through which we were looking, to remind them of the time, Wendy's mum always brought her knitting and at this stage of her life was knitting for expected grandchildren so I had to play referee. Their game, (or were they always practicing?) got under way again, Wendy darting all over the court and Tina rooted to the spot. If the shuttlecock came near her she would attempt a hit, sometimes she did succeed and crow about it to Wendy,

"That's got yer Nobby, ave won."

Well Wendy not surprisingly could not work that calculation out and seemed to forget that Tina had called her Nobby again.

If anyone is thinking that Wendy should have had a more active partner, do not worry further, as often one of the organisers would partner her, usually whilst Tina was making one of her toilet stops - and she always took her hairbrush with her so everyone knew she would be at least 10 minutes. Tina was not competitive so she wasn't unduly worried when Wendy always seemed to win, and why shouldn't she as she had done all the rushing around, even coming to Tina's side of the court to retrieve the shuttlecock, with Tina still consulting her watch or chatting to one of the organisers. Tina seemed to have all the information regarding their families and needed answers to 'as she had the baby yet' and 'oh ah' and 'wasisname' if the answer was in the affirmative. Wendy by now getting impatient and calling out to Swannee to 'urry up you', and me banging on the window to tell Swannee to hurry up you've only 10 minutes left which made Tina consult her watch again and inform Wendy and the rest of us that she was going to the toilet. And that was the end of another match. Tina and Wendy would say their goodbyes accompanied with a hug and then they would be off to their respective homes with their respective mums.

That is how it should be. Each to their own home with their own mum or other family member. Not everyone is so fortunate. To back up my statement is a depressing story, but first:-

The Gateway Club is a national organisation that started off as a social club to encourage folks with a learning disability to first access the activities there, and then to move on into the wider world of clubs, pubs, evening classes anything which the general public took for granted or their right. It was in its infancy but we managed a good turn out of members and I always stayed and helped. One night one of the young ladies who had been bussed in, asked if I would undo the fastening on her jumper at the back. I asked if it would be better if she waited until she got back home,

"No". Was the answer to that. A little group had collected around us from the same home as the young lady with the fastener problem.

"Name (which I can't remember or I would be tempted to say it) is on (duty) tonight and she wants us in bed when we get back" - a voice from the group said. This was a time in the early 1980's when it was decided by the powers that be, that it is better for people with a Learning Disability to live in small homes in the community and be a part of that small community. Amen to that I say, but the staff have to be the best, and in many many cases they were not.

I deliberately took this young lady home one night, just to see what happened when we rang the bell. I knew this staff member would be on duty and she did look surprised when she saw me as well as the young lady who lived there.

"Somebody else had to be on the bus and this is on my way home so I have given her a lift." She grunted something as to was I insured and I lied and said,

"Of course and my own daughter is in the car as well." That bit wasn't a lie.

She was very happy to come with us. "Actually she did ask me to undo her bra to help her undress quickly, would you like me to do it now she is back home?"

"No I can do it".

"Good" I said. "I told her not to worry and to always ask a member of staff. Isn't that right".

"Yes thanks for giving her a lift".

"See you next week then." I called out to the young lady.

This conversation took place without a greeting or a smile to the young lady from the staff member, she obviously knew all the rules and regulations regarding the clients, but where was the humanity? Certainly very much lacking with this worker as the residents were too terrified to ask her to help with difficult fastenings, and had to resort to asking 'anyone', as in myself, to help before they went back to their 'home' – in the community with friendly, familier staff – give me strength!

Tina was getting irritable and had opened the door and told me to 'hurry up you'.

The time is moving on at Pansy Villa and Tina is going to be a bridesmaid again! The bride this time is Karl's sister Michele and her husband to be is Nick. Tina took the whole planning of the occasion in her stride even to the measuring of the dress, and all 8 bridesmaids' dresses were to be made by Karl's mum's family. Once the measuring of Tina's vital statistics had been recorded, it became a daily ritual to say,

"Tina you must not eat crisps/biscuits/ chocolate at the ATC/college or your dress won't fit. You have been measured!"

"Alright fusspot"

Well the day dawned when Tina and I went to Michele's house to try on.

There was a lot of activity in the bedroom where the trying on of dresses was taking place. We were given a dress by Rose and after Tina had finished meeting and greeting and asking after Karl, we got down to the reason for the visit which was to try on the dress.

"Tina you will have to take your jumper and trousers off first"

"Oh alright fuss pot". She could never be bothered with trying on garments, she hated shopping and always demanded of me to 'do it.' It went over her head fine, so far so good. One arm went in with a struggle but the other refused to budge. I was panicking, Tina was becoming very irritable and kept urging me to 'hurry up you'.

I said "Tina it won't fit what have you been eating!"

"It will" said Tina but not sounding confident.

We were attracting a bit of attention now and Rose came over to help. I suddenly looked down and realised that Tina had been given the wrong dress to try on! Rose was very apologetic, Tina had been given the tallest, slimmest girl's dress, what a relief, her own dress fitted perfectly. The photo I have is faded, as it has always been on display, but I can still describe the dress. The dress, white with tiny pink flowers, was full length, fitting her perfectly, and there were frills, one from the shoulders down and around her bosom, one on the skirt part of the dress was around her knees, and the other two were around the sleeves. She has a crown on her head and her thick brown fringe is showing beneath it, she is holding a little posy bag with ribbon and has a serious expression on her face. Again we were all very proud of her.

"See" said Tina all happy now, "I didn't eat noffing". I presume she meant off the banned list.

We are still in Pansy Villa and in 1986 the improved sports centre was officially opened at the college. It had a 'proper' opening by the sports minister and Tina was part of the entertainment showing her skills on the trampoline, and how she managed to get on and jump was a mystery to us as we were only told this after the event. The photo of her is so flattering in her T shirt and track suit bottoms which were navy blue with a white stripe down the sides. When you are a college student you don't have to have family with you. Tina is really branching out, she is 27ish

A significant happening at Pansy Villa was the introduction of someone who became known as Tina's best mate - not my husband. The best mate and I were forced on each other by an over zealous ex sister in law, we didn't click, or get to know each other for a long time, but we obviously did as we were married very quietly on Tina's 29th birthday (the day before my 47th if anyone is interested.) We partied in the afternoon and the first to know was Tina and she cheered and told the rest of the families when they came for her birthday.*

Let us end this chapter on a happy occasion. And the occasion will be Tina's 30th birthday and party. However we have someone else to meet first who most definitely can't be left out.

Rachel (the dignified sister) was a member of the Gilbert and Sullivan society which produced a show with very lively music as is the norm for G and S. Tina and I would go to support the production and became quite

---

* Tina had a friend for the rest of her life. The sad fact was, the year of our 25th wedding anniversary was the first after Tina's death and we did nothing at all to celebrate. How could we when Tina was not with us anymore to celebrate her birthday and take the attention from us! But we are not there yet.

This reminds me that the first Mothers Day after Teresa's death was the day which should have been her birthday. Life can kick you quite hard in the teeth at times.

friendly with some of the people, but we didn't meet the conductor of the orchestra until one day Rachel asked if she could bring 'someone' home for tea. Well of course I wanted to know some details as I had guessed that Rachel had a boy friend and his name was John, rather a difficult word for Tina to pronounce. 'he eats anything mum,' answered my food question

I decided to cook something in the slow cooker, Tina had been warned not to ask Goch - her pronunciation of John - for his CV, so we were ready and in came Rachel and Goch. John had a Yorkshire accent, coming from Sheffield, he seemed quite shy and just answered the questions that I asked him so the conversation didn't move very quickly until....!!! Rachel was setting the table, I was deciding if the slow cooker had done it's job and cooked our dinner and on opening the top slowly I was met with a burst of food onto my chest. Yes it was hot! Well I was sent into the bathroom to 'take your clothes off mum, I'll help you' from Rachel, Tina had taken over setting the table, John was rooted to the chair and looked rather forlorn. I suppose he was thinking, well I won't get any tea now, actually there was quite a lot in the pan which was reasonably sufficient. Since then this event has been discussed at every gathering when the slow cooker is used.

John stuck it out with us and like the 'best mate' bonded with Tina, taking her after cricket to the Red Cat pub in North Wootton where the bones of the match were being dissected by the team. Tina meeting and greeting in her usual way and adding their CV's to her list.

Now back to the birthday party arrangements:-

We decided that it would be a surprise party and so when Tina was asking 'what am a doing. It's ma birthday yknow."

How could we forget.

"Would you like to go to the Chinese Tina" asked the Rachel.

"Yes a would" quickly replied Tina. "Who's coming".

"Well, you tell us who you would like to come and Mum will sort it out, but don't tell anyone Tina because that will be a nice surprise."

This is becoming complicated. Tina mustn't know about her surprise party and the guests mustn't think that they are going to the Chinese because nobody is going to the Chinese, everyone will go to the Blue and

Gold club at the side of the Lynn Walks. We had about two weeks to plan and keep quiet.

Sheila made a super cake for Tina, not a sausage pie, and another for us, because 'it is your anniversary'. I thought Tina will not like that.

It was decided that Rachel and her now fiancée Goch, would do the transporting of Tina to the Blue and Gold club whilst we went early to make sure that everything was ready when the guests arrived. We would all be waiting and then burst into 'Happy Birthday' on her arrival. The best laid plans...... It was getting late and the birthday girl with entourage had not arrived. The baby sister (who is now 14) went outside with a friend to see if there were any signs of the little group. No. We were not sure what to do when suddenly the door opened and the escorts entered with a slightly reluctant Tina who had refused to get out of the car because 'I'm not walking to the Chinese from here'! She looked bemused for a few seconds and then her face lit up as the 'penny had dropped'.

She had a wonderful time which was a relief because she did like to go to the Chinese and it could have gone so horribly wrong, but Tina did not like us having our anniversary cake and the singing of Happy Anniversary by her guests and she said,

"I got you a card dint I?"

And every year yes she did but not a birthday card for me. That was left to one of the sisters to organise on her behalf of course.

Well Pansy Villa was sold, the best mate's house was going on the market, but in the meantime, for a short while, we were going to Massingham!

Tina in her bridesmaid dress at Michele's wedding – Michele was Karl's sister.

Celebrating at the surprise 30th birthday party.

This is Tina's 30th birthday 'surprise' party at the Blue and Gold club. Rachel and John brought her to the club in the car. Tina refused to get out because she thought she was going for a Chinese meal and she was not going to walk! She was thrilled when she went into the room and saw all the people and a very good time was had by everyone!

Tina was finally taught to swim at Lake Bled by a wonderful instructor who pulled her along the lake until she was confident enough to let go.

What a scoop to swim with Duncan Goodhew, the Olympic swimming champion. This was at Gunton Hall, a holiday camp in Suffolk.

Tina joining in a game of water polo with the lovely chaps in Southern Spain.

She is enjoying the slide in our swimming pool –
Tina was in her late twenties at the time.

This is Grandma with Tina, she would have been with us over the Christmas holiday. Also it would have been Rachel's birthday.

Butlins SWIMATHON

17 - 23 March 2003

www.swimathon.org

Butlins Swimathon 2003, PO Box 30775, London WC1B 4QE
tel: 0845 36 700 36 (local rate) **fax:** 020 7745 3301
email: info@swimathon.org

24 April 2003

Christina Swann
18 Castle Acre Road
Great Massingham
KING S LYNN PE32 2HD

Entry Number: 140639

Dear Christina

A VERY BIG THANK YOU ...

for sending us your sponsorship money to Butlins Swimathon 2003. This is an amazing achievement and everyone at Butlins Swimathon is very grateful to you!

Tina's very big thank you from Butlin's swimathon.

13

Great Massingham

Best laid plans sometimes take a different turn. Going to live in Massingham was something I would never have contemplated, was it too far out of King's Lynn for Tina's services, would she manage to catch the bus in the bus station?

Key worker Val, in whom we had great faith, was very helpful and positive as to Tina's ability to cope. She organised a bus pass which would enable her to travel from home into King's Lynn, then to catch another bus to South Wootton, a mile and a half in distance from the town centre, to the home for the elderly called Woodlands – 'Wuggerlands' in Tina speak - where Tina 'worked' for two days per week, of which more later!

Going back slightly in time, Tina finished her education at the Alderman Jackson School which she thoroughly enjoyed, even with her last teacher, a Mrs Reed, who was quite firm! Her reading skills improved immensely, and she managed to read the TV Times for the times of her favourite programmes. Mrs Reed's firmness had paid off and Tina's achievements were wonderful to see and hear.

So Tina has left that behind and is now finishing her education at the Adult Training Centre (ATC). It had a philosophy of equality so all could try the various leisure activities and work options, e.g. woodwork, gardening and oh dear, concreting. These included painting, drawing, sewing, and knitting, which may not have been the route into employment but they were skills that helped the flexibility of the hands and, as important, gave satisfaction. The more hardy people could play football at break times, and there was a choir which was organised by Jane, who years later I met up with at the Big Heart and Soul Choir, of which I am still a member.

I remember going to a concert at the ATC to hear the choir sing and was immediately transported back to the Orchard St School in Dewsbury which Tina attended, listening to the young people singing with so much enthusiasm. Tina did not sing in either choir and when I asked her why not, she just said rather rudely that it was crap!

So although there were lots of things to do at the ATC, I have the feeling that Tina bluffed her way around it all. Her favourite occupation seemed to be hanging round the kitchen hatch (that sounds a bit harsh.) But if that was her favourite, her least favourite was the concreting area. The skin on her hands was becoming very red and sore. Something would have to be done as Tina had said that she would leave unless she could stop concreting. So I went to complain, the supervisors had been far too rigid in my opinion, and I think they realised this when Tina showed them her hands, so she moved out of that department. What were they making you might ask? I did not even enquire!

Tina was an absolutely social person and really enjoyed the opportunities to go away for a week with the ATC. One holiday was to Gunton Hall in Suffolk with the Olympic swimmer Duncan Goodhew in attendance, so Tina must have her picture taken with him - and she did.

Did the staff have a break at the end? I wondered.

Tina is now spending more time at Woodlands – 'Wuggerlands' - and her time at the then technical college was most productive, delicious cakes travelled home on the bus, and were hidden in her bedroom until the best mate came home.

This was becoming a very happy settled time in her life, but in the 1990's I was asked if Tina would like to join a new project by the name of NORCI STEP. This initiative was shared between Norfolk and the EU, money had been given and must be used. It was another attempt to try and secure work places for people with learning disabilities and Tina, who liked something new as long as she could still go to Wuggerlands, was up for it. She did go to see some of the other work places on offer, but her heart wasn't really in it. She just went for the cup of coffee.

One thing that did change for Tina was that she was not invited to the ATC's Christmas party! The reason being, explained an embarrassed receptionist, was that she was not registered there anymore. I contacted the local press to see if they wanted an unChristmas story and they did. Of course I had to pick up the flack from all this, as a picture of Tina and myself plus an account had been printed in the paper, so I was 'invited' to a meeting at the centre.

Why had I not spoken to them first, was their opening comment. To which I replied that I had spoken to the receptionist who had gone to check with a senior person, who had said that the information given to me was correct and Tina was not invited. So I rested my case. I was very angry on Tina's behalf and I felt I was in the right to inform the press. The majority of people were on my side, feeling that it was a miserly thing to do, especially at Christmas. Nobody had said that she couldn't go to a Christmas party because of her involvement with NORCI STEP - perhaps there was a secret, sinister side to it! Well Tina had had enough and milked the situation where ever we went, and so everyone soon knew that she had missed a Christmas party.

It is not easy for people with a learning disability to make and keep friendships, so a party at Christmas is, or should be, a perfect time to get together and socialise without a family member or helpers, giving them a bit of space, like any other adult, to have fun with their friends. The Gateway Club held every other Monday was a brilliant example of enabling people to get together and have a jolly good time, and long may it continue. Tina was always greeted with big hugs and had a special friend in Jamie he and his family became friends with us all.

Shall we go to Wuggerlands now and have an insight into Tina's time there?

She would set the tables for lunch having to remember who sat where, and particularly two people who preferred to sit on their own. On one occasion when Alan and Audrey (A and A) were visiting from their home in Bradford, we went to Wuggerlands to view Tina's table setting. Tina was thrilled, and had actually mentioned on various occasions that she would like someone to see her work. Of course I asked for permission first, and we arrived as per directed before the lunch was served and

Tina and Pat* were standing at the side of a table, and A and A walked around making complimentary remarks, Tina quietly just moving a knife a fraction and then stepping away, I was so near to tears. She absolutely loved being there and showing to her friends what she had done was enlightening and encouraging. Most people like their work to be admired and Tina certainly fitted into that category. How true is the statement that 'everybody can do something'.

Tina's next job of the day would be to help clear the tables and wash up. On these days she was working/chatting/drinking coffee/eating her lunch with the other kitchen workers, listening to the gossip of families, weddings, births sometimes deaths, and the next episode of East Enders (according to the staff.)

On her return home she would relay the conversations to the best mate and myself and whoever else was around to listen. So we heard of incidents in these peoples' lives both great and small (I hoped that the spreading of the minutiae of the lives of people to us by Tina was acceptable. I am sure ours would also have been passed around.)

Tina and I are now leading parallel lives in our new abode with Tony, the best mate/husband.

The rest of this story will take place in Great Massingham,** and the events I am about to describe, will scan the next 10 years of Tina's life where she will still be the old Tina. The new Tina will be hovering around the corner of her life where the condition of dementia will be waiting to pounce like a dreaded fiend into her unsuspecting brain.

But we are not there yet. Let us enjoy, as the eternal triangle we have become, our life in Great Massingham.

Do I hear shouts of 'I thought you were moving'?

---

* Pat is a lady who worked at Wuggerlands who had taken Tina under her wing and given her a little support. When Val came to check on Tina (to keep her records straight) she would chat to Pat with regards to Tina's behaviour and ability. Tina loved Pat. I was pleased that Pat had met A and A, something to talk about at the lunch time sessions.

** I do not regard the uncare home as a place where Tina lived.

Correct! However the estate agent who came to view the property thought it would be a good idea if the garden could be landscaped, making it a more attractive offer and helping it reach its full market potential. There was three quarters of an acre to play around with, mostly grass, which was acceptable when the best mate's children were growing up. Time moved on and garden fever set in.

'Do you 'ave to' Tina would wail if we paused on a shopping trip to make a detour to a garden centre.

'We won't be long, why don't you come in with us. I think there is a coffee shop'.

And Tina would be out of the car like the proverbial bullet out of a gun - well not quite, we are talking languid mover Tina.

If there was a coffee shop great. If not Tina and her best mate would be disappointed and Tina, in her loudest voice, would announce that she was going 'to the toilet'.

'Am desperate y'naw'.

Well I think the message has been received by the readers of this, Tina was as interested in the garden and whatever her mother was buying for it, as she was about her mother's singing which will be explained further!

Still talking outdoor activities - Tina had been given an operation to remove a varicose vein and the aftercare included walking three miles every day! To start with I accompanied Tina and we planned out a route which would take us along part of the disused airfield. She was not happy with this arrangement as she never liked being accompanied by me. Again it was a blow to her independence, but I remained firm and lied a bit by saying that I had been advised to go with her. On one occasion I was very relieved to have been on the walk with Tina, I was in front with Tina trailing behind, and on turning round to see if she was catching me up I saw a huge plane with no sound coming from it just quietly approaching Tina. She was in the middle of the runway! I did not dare to speak loudly why? Tina then turned round saw the plane and waved at the pilot and friend, Tina thinking that it was just part of the walk. I was shaking and made up my mind never to allow her to walk on her own, which was a difficult thing for her to accept. But we did keep impressing on her that the air field was a difficult place, private planes were also allowed to share the space, and it was a long walk, and she did not need to go all that way.

I don't think that three miles was always covered so a very kind relative bought her a stop watch, proof indeed. However the specialist was satisfied with her progress so to quote Tina it was "Good job an all", and we were all relieved. We did find out later that when she had finally shaken me off her walks, Tina had stopped off at "Sunday morning Jeanne and Ant's" house on several occasions, which would include a cup of coffee and biscuits, and then on arriving home would sink into the sofa claiming that she was knackered.

After her visit to Jeanne and Ant's on Sunday mornings she would come home for her lunch, and if nothing much was going to be happening in the afternoon she would slip off to Hazel's house which was on the other side of the duck pond. There she would have a cup of tea (Tina didn't drink tea at home, she was probably being polite) and a biscuit. I am not sure when Hazel and Tina got together, but in the mornings they would meet at the bus stop by the church and travel together to the hospital car park, where Hazel would get off the bus and Tina would carry on to the bus station. Hazel worked in one of the canteens at the hospital, and going home they would meet up on the bus.

However, a 'little bird' in the form of a friend from the village visiting the hospital, said that on their last visit Tina had been seen working with Hazel. Tina was loading the trolley with the used cups and saucers, was she on the pay roll I thought, but Tina in her usual way would have thought that it was the right thing to do to help her friend.

One evening we had a phone call from Hazel's mum with the sad announcement that Hazel would not be catching the bus the next day as she had died, and she didn't want Tina to be wondering where she was. We knew that Hazel walked with a limp but we knew nothing about her general health, and it was so thoughtful of her mum thinking of Tina and feeling the urgency to let us know. We did have to tell Tina this news and I asked her if she would like the best mate to take her to Woodlands.

"No I'm going on the bus."

"Hazel won't be there love,"

"A know that mum."

We must move on to an 'outing' with another friend and, unfortunately for Tina, me. I was to accompany them to a special event - the pageant to celebrate the Queen Mother's 100th birthday!

Val, the key worker, had asked me if I would take Tina and her friend Margaret to London to join the celebrations, and I thought, 'through rose coloured glasses', that it was a lovely opportunity for them to represent West Norfolk Mencap. Anyway I agreed, and on the morning of 19th July 2000 AD the three of us set off on the train.

Travelling with Tina with or without friends could always provoke a reaction from fellow travellers; some will stare steadfastly ahead as if remembering what they had been taught as a child, 'don't stare it's rude' even though Tina has started to ask questions in her loud voice; some are sitting quietly reading; some are making a lot of noise themselves and are drowning Tina's questions out; some I could see were enjoying the diversion. Margaret meanwhile sits quietly.

Right this is it folks, we have reached our station, out we stepped and made our way to the exit for the Golden Lane area. All good so far, but what a let down when we found it, and then the Mencap office, making 3 'd's', dull, drab and disappointing.

I walked up to the reception in the Mencap office and was stared at, no, I mean glared at, by the lady behind said desk. She said she did not know anything about the pageant until she had arrived at work, there wasn't room in there for us to wait until the bus came to pick us up and take us to St James Park, and we were told to go and wait outside on the pavement. She did not give Tina or Margaret a smile or any type of acknowledgement, and she was working for Mencap! Did she really not know that we, and the other people who were also gathering on the pavement, had made a long journey after being invited by Mencap to take part in the parade?

The bus arrived to take us to St James Park, 'don't get on yet' the driver ordered. These were people with multiple disabilities, so some had to stand, and some sat on the floor and it was becoming hotter. This appalling treatment was shocking from a charity which had the Queen Mother as its patron, which was supposed to try and make life easier for the learning disabled and their families and be championing their rights. I gave up!

At last we were allowed to get on the bus, the journey wasn't too far, then Margaret and Tina changed into their green overall type pinafore work clothes as per instructions and joined at number 10 in the parade. There were massed bands galore, the Red Arrows, the Philharmonic Orchestra and a choir, which was made up of a few choirs all singing together, and the Chicken Shed theatre company whose slogan was 'Excellence without Exclusion' and was open to all children throughout the country - I hope that they are still performing - and then a special birthday song for Her Majesty.

It was all so impressive but exhausting at the same time. Margaret and Tina managed most of the procession and they were helped by a smiling lady from Mencap, hurrah - a smiling pleasant lady. When they were returned to me, it was pointed out that a lady sitting on a bale of hay was an actress in Coronation St. Tina, suddenly tiredness forgotten, was the proverbial bullet and rushed over to start her interrogation. I left her for about five minutes to enjoy being alone with her, and then started to wander over as Tina would have never moved. She said goodbye, and we all left to catch the train home. The highlights of Tina's day was meeting the actress and a meal voucher, and I know it would have been a more enjoyable and relaxed occasion if more people we knew had attended.

Talking of events, our garden party was to be a small affair, for people attending the ATC and their families, to raise money for a swimming pool at the ATC. Everyone enjoyed themselves, and it was suggested that we should have another. Well we did have this big garden and the socialist nature of me came out and I thought that the garden plus swimming pool should be shared, but if you think of a ball rolling down a hill gathering speed, that is how our event grew and evolved and it is still going today!

It just became a huge attraction and was very well attended by the ATC of course, the school where Tina helped out once a year, there was music from a DJ, a helper at the Junior Gateway Club, and the Big Heart and Soul Choir, to which I belonged, came and sang. The villagers came with cakes etc that were homemade, and most of mine and Tony's (best mate's) families, so in short 'Uncle Tom Cobley and All.' The swimming pool was open with strict instructions to parents that they were responsible for their own children. Notices were everywhere. We did have a lifeguard trained person at the pool. And lots of friends making the drinks - no alcohol allowed.

Now you might be thinking was Tina involved? Well nothing was ever said but people did wonder where she was.

Tina was choosing her moment.

Suddenly she appeared in her swimming costume and walked slowly towards the pool, people stepping aside to let her pass. It was similar to the parting of the waves and then - drum roll - she was in. Head down and away she went. Five minutes, then she was out and back in her room. I followed her and spoke through a closed door asking if she was coming back out.

"A'm having a shower."

"Shall we see you later then Tina."

"If I must she replied."

Tina usually participated in her way, meeting and greeting who she did know and asking for information from the people who she did not know - in short being friendly - except to keep telling one and all that her mother could not sing and why was she in the choir?

That was Tina before dementia started it's attack on her brain, when she knew what she was doing, as in waiting for the right moment for the maximum attention before she entered the water.

The very last time she came to the garden party was with two carers from the uncare home. The top she was wearing was dirty and the carers showed their non caring attitude by keeping her separate from the groups. They were out of their comfort zone and did not know how to mix. I found a top for Tina to wear and helped them to put it on her. She was admitted to hospital quite soon after that.

The good and the bad times one might say. Fortunately the good times were greater than the bad.

For our family there was some wonderful news, Louise, the baby sister, was pregnant.

Rachel and John's Wedding
August 4th 1990

It is nearly time for Tina to take on the role of a bridesmaid again. And a chief bridesmaid as well. So a very important time for Tina. Sister Louise and John's niece Kirstie were the other two bridesmaids.

Choosing of the dresses seemed to be quite easy. They were from Laura Ashley, so 'off the peg' one might say, and all the girls looked lovely in them. So there was a task completed. The shoes I have to admit, or were they sandals, mm possibly, were bought independently. I presume I took Tina. Do you remember that Tina doesn't like buying anything new, having to try things on, mother hovering and making sure things fitted?

"But Tina your shoes/sandals have to fit properly, you can't walk down the aisle following Rachel if your shoes don't fit"

"Alright fuss pot." Meaning she has accepted the situation.

We could go for a coffee afterwards, I offer.

On a lovely picture of the wedding party the bridesmaids' were all wearing white shoes with a tiny kitten heel. Very popular at the time. So that was the answer to the footwear. The headdresses and posies were made by Susan, a florist and school friend of Rachel's all looking beautifully positioned.

Rachel looked stunning in her dress which was made and bought from a proper wedding shop.

On this occasion, Tina fitted into her dress perfectly, Louise's had to have a slight alteration.

The day dawned and the weather looked very promising. It was also the Queen mother's 90th birthday, so good weather was very welcome for that occasion also.

Everybody got to the church on time, and all went to plan during the service, the bridesmaids and the two little page boys in their sailor suits were given a pew to sit in. Tina doing her usual sit when everyone is standing and then the reverse. Perhaps Louise encouraged her to sit with a little tug on her arm.

Now Tina's big moment is coming:- The smaller version of the bridal party were taken into the vestry for the signing of the wedding documents, Tina being the chief bridesmaid had, as a witness, to sign her name. And she did 'to perfection' Rachel said. What a relief.

After that it was all out of the church, Rachel now a married woman, confetti flying, pictures were taken, and again, and again, and then as they the bride and groom, Mr and Mrs Mellor, moved off, Rachel paused at the grave of her sister Teresa and placed her flowers there. A sobering gesture for a few moments for us all.

We are now all in the Dukes Head on the Tuesday market place in King's Lynn and Tina is ready for the party to start.

The speeches first, Tina.

Tina did not have to speak so she rather politely listened to all the speeches which were not very long, so she clapped and laughed in the correct places

One lovely thing for us was to have my mum with us. Mum was rather shy and quiet most of the time but as I have said earlier she could do fantastic impressions but not in front of other people. She loved the wedding but did find it rather overwhelming.

Back to Tina

She has already made friends with the musicians, friends of John, from Uni. I am not sure if the musicians played all night something else to ask Rachel.

The next day Rachel and John set off on their honeymoon, a journey down the Nile (Tony's present for them), and the guests who had stayed over in King's Lynn came and partied again, christening the 'just finished' swimming pool. Tina being in life and soul mood and demonstrating how to swim 'underneath'

So there we are, and that was the last of Tina's bridesmaid days.

The next couples' right of passage would be Louise and Spencer's wedding and Tina will 'Give the bride away'.

Not Yet.

Tina is forty and celebrating with flowers and cakes. One of the cakes was made by Sheila and the other by her friend's Grandma.

Celebrating Tina's 40th birthday. She is with Mickey Mouse and young friends. Tina made a wonderful speech!

Holiday and party times with family.

We are on holiday in Tunisia. Tina is always the first to volunteer!

Tina stepping carefully off the plane – Salou was 'the pits'.

Swimming in Florida with Mum and Rachel.

Visiting Scotland – the 1st stop.

Tina taking Rachel on a walk up Mount Snowden, Tina fell in a bog! When they reached the top they had no money to buy refreshments and souvenirs from the mountain top shop.

Outside Downing Street. How did Tina manage to stand on a bollard and take a picture!

Is it your birthday Tina or is it Christmas?

Will she like it? Look at the other picture.

On pilgrimage in Jerusalem, from left to right is Josette, Sheila and Tina.

Tina's 31st birthday spent in Jerusalem. The beautiful cake was made by the hotel's cook.

A very cold day In Germany with Tina on the roundabout. Is Tina wearing my hat?

Tina and Rachel at Louise's graduation.

Enjoying a cuddle from Louise on graduation day.

Tina pictured in 1996 at Woodlands Care Home where she worked for 28 years.*
**It was always 'Wuggerlands' to use Tina's pronunciation.*

Tina and Pat at Woodlands in 2000.

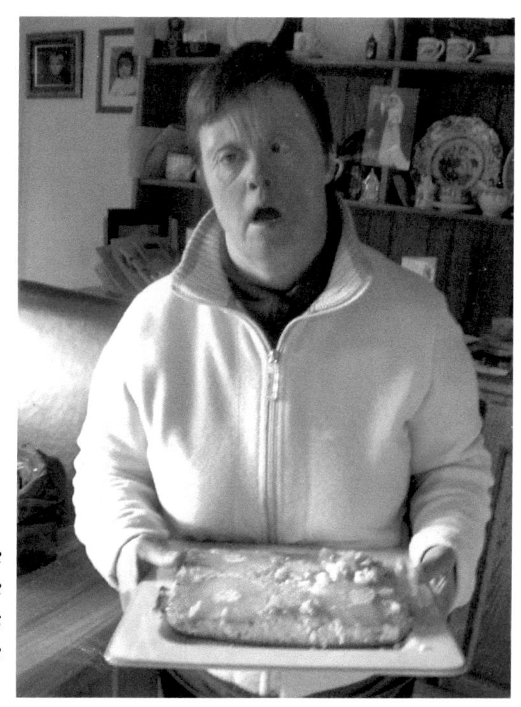

This is Tina aged 47 with the 'pineapple upside-down' cake that she cooked for us. This was probably the last cake that she cooked.

Partying with Margaret on the left and Wendy on the right.

Mencap Holiday weekend. Tina is waiting with Jamie to be hoisted – she didn't go!

Is it Easter time Tina? You are wearing a very busy hat.

Coffee time with 'Sunday Morning' Jeanne and Ant. Tina is a regular visitor.

Tina, the chief bridesmaid at her sister's wedding three times now! She is having a quiet few minutes.

14

Still at Wuggerlands

Running alongside Tina at Wuggerlands was Tina at Tom Thumb Play Group where she went on Tuesday after her table setting session. The play group was situated opposite the school in Marsh Lane where she had attended as a pupil, and made official visits to while she was still at the school, to see how she would fit in if in the future she would like to help out on a more permanent basis. What was not to like for Tina? There was coffee at break time and what goes with coffee? Correct, biscuits! There were people who could fill in their CV's for her and of course there were children, who she did enjoy.

Although Tina was wiser and had had more experience of life, some of the children were educationally in front of Tina, but she was street wise, she travelled by bus, and could set the tables for lunch at Wuggerlands! The children, on the other hand could speak more clearly and generally their development would be continuing whereas Tina's would be beginning to slow down, but here we are now and she is enjoying what she is doing, so long may it continue I say.

If Tina was in one of her diet modes she would walk down to the play group, the distance being about a mile. (I hope she was wearing her pedometer). Once there and after her greetings to everyone, and possibly drinking a coffee, she would be given a small task or two with the children, perhaps she would draw or paint with them or glue something? She was rather vague when asked what she had been doing.

'Not much' she sometimes said, but other times she would be eager to tell me what one child had been doing. All the children seemed to take

Tina in their stride, sometimes her speech could be confusing, and there was usually another adult to help out. Gradually they became so used to her and her speech that they thought nothing of it and perhaps helped their parents out by translating what she has said, just as my family, almost automatically, have been the translators.

In the summer our Mencap would use the Alderman Jackson school to have a week of activities for the children who attended AJ's, similar to their schooling but with other activities, and every group would go on a trip. The beach hut belonging to Mencap at old Hunstanton was a favourite place to go, it was almost on the beach, and lunch could be eaten either in or outside the hut depending on the weather.

Now where does Tina fit into this arrangement? She took a week off work at Woodlands and we travelled together and then parted company at the door of the school.

"See you later Tina have a good day."

She did not bother to reply, she was off. Tina was helping with the youngest children and I with the oldest and that suited Tina very well, if we had been together she would not have volunteered. Remember her space. However one day I had just popped into the break room for a coffee to see Tina still in there clutching left over biscuits.

'Shouldn't you be with your group Tina' I asked.

'A'm going now' she said, and hurried off.

I didn't get the chance to ask how things were going.

On the last day we had a concert and drawings or things made with plasticine were on view. Some of the older children made scrap books about the places they had been, and they were so proud to show them off and have them admired. The singing started, individuals first then each group and then we would all sing together. It was really lovely and again a good time was had by all. Tina had found a little friend and was sad when the last day came.

"I am sure she will be here next year Tina."

Spiky Mike one of the leaders at the play group was a favourite of Tina's, in short she had a crush on him. She insisted on referring to his wife as his ex girl friend, so when this lady produced a baby and she and baby were going to come and visit the play group I did wonder what Tina's reactions would be. Evidently everything went well Tina held the baby and told us all about her experience when she came home. I suggested we looked for a present, 'I'll do it myself' she said. I think she must have forgotten, but she did sign her name on a joint card.

Sometimes she would try and sneak off from play group early but Spiky Mike always insisted that her job was to wash the paint brushes before she departed. I was pleased that as she was being treated like an adult with a job to perform before she left.*

On leaving after a loud 'bye Tina' from the children she would catch the bus into town and, surprise surprise, end up in the King Burger before catching the bus home.**

So we will leave the play group now and in our thoughts follow Tina into the King Burger, where she had her afternoon drink(s) before catching the bus home. Tina seemed to have her own table and would discard her possessions on and around it including her handbag. Someone had shopped her to me as she had left them to nip to the toilet, and I would try to tell her,

'Don't do that Tina, keep your bag with you, someone might take it.'

'They won't, she said. Tina has to learn safety of possessions rules, a bit harsh for someone as trusting as her!

However something did happen one day. I am surmising that Tina must have done her usual, gone upstairs to the toilet, leaving her bag on her table, and when she came down it was gone. Her phone and bus pass were

---

* Spiky Mike and partner did come to one of Tina's 50th birthday parties with the rest of the play group staff, but we are not there yet.

** Sometimes Tina, on finishing her coffee and going outside the café, would perhaps meet someone that we both knew and the following conversation would commence with a discussion on where had they been, where do they work, is it nice there etc, etc. I also did find out that if she saw someone smoking outside the café and she knew them, and they had not hidden the offending cigarette behind their back then she would be onto them like a ton of bricks with, "Smoking again! It's bad for you. Give it up" and with that advice she would be off. So like my dad.

the major items which she needed to get home, her purse had disappeared as well, she was in quite a panic. The staff were wonderful and phoned to give me the sad, to Tina devastating, news. Oh Tina what have we been telling you? I phoned the 'best mate' and he went to collect, a very sad lady who cried all the way home.*

Had a salutary lesson been learnt? One day I was in the town and thought I would just glance into the Kingburger and see if Tina looked alright. By this time she had received a new bus pass, the phone, purse and bag had been replaced. I looked round but couldn't see her. What I could see was the new bag on the table but not with the owner. Suddenly she is there back from the toilet and I say between clenched teeth

"Tina you left your bag!"

"S'alright mum 'av got my bus pass in ma pocket. What you doing 'ere.?"

"I was just passing, I'll see you later."

Tina's wish for independence led to some difficulties, and she always did her best to steer me away from 'interfering' with her life outside of home. On one occasion I had to take my car into the garage for a service, and leave it over night, and when I got home after tea I informed Tina and the best mate that I would be 'catching your bus Tina'. Tina left the room and went into her bedroom, no doubt to absorb this piece of news. She came back looking quite jubilant,

"I Know, Why don't you ask Tone (best mate) to bring you back?"

"Well Tina I don't think that will be necessary as he comes home later, and I would like to get back and start cooking our tea. Anyway it will be nice to catch the bus with you."

No reply from you know who. She disappears again.

"I know." She has bounced back. "Why don't you go to Rachel's (dig sis) work and come back with her? She'll bring you back."

---

* The bag was found near Sainsbury's. Purse, bus pass and money gone. Tina received a booklet from the police advising her on keeping her possessions safe.

"No Tina I can't do that. I wouldn't be allowed in and anyway why can't I come on your bus?

"You 'avn't got a bus pass."

"Well I will have some money so I can pay."

"You can't it's for 'tec students."

This ping pong went on all evening, with a break for East Enders, and then she announced that she would think about it.

I didn't raise the subject again, best to let her think that I had changed my mind. She was quite disturbed about it which made me think was something going on but, as I have repeatedly thought and said out loud, I do like Tina to have some control of her own affairs and not always having someone telling her what to and what not to do. Mostly this arrangement works, but occasionally it wobbles. An example was when I arrived early to meet her at the building society in the town, only to see her coming out with notes clamped in her lips, whilst she was opening her bag.

"Why didn't you wait for me?" I asked, releasing the notes from her mouth. "You mustn't put money in your mouth Tina you don't know where it's been."

"I do," she said, "in there."

Anyway I am going to catch the bus:-

When I arrived at the bus stop the queue hadn't started to form. I looked round and saw Tina with 1 or 2 people and I managed to catch her eye and give her a wave. She stared or rather glared, and looked away. One girl said

"Tina your mum's there."

"I know that. A've seen er."

"Is she coming on the bus with you?"

"Yes, worse luck."

"Oh don't say that Tina, she's nice is your mum."

Tina didn't answer that as the bus had just arrived.

Now we are in a line and walking slowly towards the entrance. Tina, who was just in front of me has done her stepping out, walking slowly and moving in next to someone she knew. We are all on the move again and Tina has performed the side stepping manoeuvre, again moving until she comes to the steps of the bus and of course a nice person makes way for her to get in first. So there she is sitting on the front seat watching the rest of us get on. When I had drawn level with the empty space next to her she looked at me and said quite clearly,

"I sit here on my own."

"Oh alright Tina where should I sit?" she pointed vaguely behind on the opposite side to her.

Well we are just about to move off when a lady comes rushing towards the door and scrambles on and looks at the seat next to Tina.

"Hello Tina," Tina smiles back, "Can I sit here" she says,

"Course you can" Tina replies.

The bus moves off and Tina and her fellow passenger are having a little conversation, most likely Tina will be wanting to know what she has been doing today and where is her husband. She may have gone into question mode and asked the lady what she was having for her tea. Perhaps the lady had asked what was she having, and at that point Tina turned to ask me, and the lady looked round and sounding very apologetic asked if she had taken my seat.

"Oh no," says I, "Tina likes to sit with different people. You are fine there."

By this time we are at the college bus stop and the students start to crowd onto the bus. A few acknowledge Tina, as perhaps they have seen her around. Then I suddenly have a young lady, who I recognise from our village, sitting next to me.

"Your Tina's mum aren't you?"

"Yes I am" of course I reply.

"Where is she then?" she says looking round.

"She's sitting at the front next to that lady, can you see her?"

"Yes but why isn't she sitting with you?"

"She wanted to be by herself."

"Tina," shouts the young lady (and she has a very loud voice), "why didn't you want to sit with your mum?"

The whole bus went quiet, probably waiting for Tina's reply - and what about the poor lady sitting next to her, what is she feeling like? She could have been making a mental note to not be late for the bus again, and I was making a similar mental note to not get on Tina's bus again.

It was not just me - Tony, the best mate, being without a car one day decided to catch Tina's bus. He was dispatched to the back of the bus, and like myself he decided not to do that again!

The one and only time that I was allowed into the bus station was to take Tina a bag of clothes as she was going to spend the weekend with Louise in Norwich. Louise would be in the bus station where the bus would stop and discharge the passengers and I spoke to the driver and say that Tina was going all the way to Norwich bus station and would be met by her sister. The staff always nodded to me as in recognition of their vulnerable passenger. I stood near to the bus to wave Tina off, which she seemed to accept, and she then produced a bag of crisps and proceeded to eat them, smiling at me whilst she did so!

Tina's journey home was often eventful. Do you remember the delicious cakes which arrived home with Tina in a box in her bag? Well they were not the only things arriving home with Tina. If she had bought a present or even a card for someone and the best mate or I was home before her (remember she does have her own key), we would be instructed to, 'don't look', and she would rush off into her bedroom with the surprise. If it was something in her bag then she could continue with the secrecy and view... whatever at her leisure. If the surprise was for 'the best mate', then I would be ordered into her room and 'shut the door' command was issued so she could show me. If it was for me then, yes you guessed it, the item was shown to best mate. We have a collection of items which will always be with us, he very delicate cup and saucer with the word 'September ' on it was for one of the best mate's birthdays which is in June! I have 'love you mum' on a tiny vase with a red rose in it given to me for a mother's day. It is on the window sill in my bedroom and the September cup and saucer are on the unit in the dining /kitchen area.

Now a bunch of flowers or even a plant arriving with Tina are more difficult to disguise, and as she couldn't really open the door with these items, so she thuds on the door with her body calling out 'open the door', sometimes it would turn into a 'bloody door', and 'don't look'. So find your way to the door, open it keeping your eyes tight shut and in she comes and hurries into her room. We wouldn't hear any more until I remembered to ask the best mate if, whatever had been brought home, needed water, or even air if it had been tightly packed. If that sounded difficult to manage then think of a small tree or bush. Keep that in your mind whilst I give some details.

Tina had taken it upon herself to ask the bus driver if he would stop the bus at the end of Lynn Lane as she did not want to walk back from the correct stop as it was about 100 metres in the opposite direction to our house. Most drivers were compliant with this order/request, however one stuck to the rules of not allowing passengers to leave the bus until at a correct stop. Tina did grumble if he was the driver.

"Tina he is just doing his job, if you had an accident he would be in serious trouble for letting you get off."

"Like Grandma?"

"Well something like that, but that won't happen to you."

I wish I hadn't brought up the painful fact of my mum crossing a road getting knocked down, and dying from her injuries. It was a very distressing time for all of us, she was mine and my brother's mum and grandma to her 6 grand daughters. She had played a huge role in all our lives over the years especially Tina's. Bearing this in mind, during the darker evenings either the best mate or myself would walk to where Tina asked to be let off, then if the bus carried on to the official stop we hurried along until we met.

One day, suddenly there was thundering and shouting going on outside the door, was my watch or the clock wrong? Oh no Tina's walked back and there is hardly any light, I couldn't open the door so I presumed she was leaning against it.

"Tina can you move away from the door love, I can't open it as you are leaning on it."

"Shut yer eyes," she had changed tack.

"Alright I've got them shut, can you move a bit now?"

She did, and of course I had opened my eyes and saw not just Tina but Tina looking as if she was dressed like a tree, branches with leaves and a thick stem all encased into a large pot..

"How have you managed to carry …. ?"

"Shut yer eyes mum it's a secret!"

Well the 'secret' is still with us in a corner of the lounge very near to where the memory butterfly hangs in the winter months. (This was made for us by Caroline a lovely lady who I met through the choir.)

Let us go back into the day and think of her outward journey to Wuggerlands, although appearing to go smoothly they could have a drama attached. How long this drama had been enacted we never found out. Now it started with one day Tina had to accept me taking her to the dentist as she had an early appointment and then taking her to Wuggerlands. We had to have quite a discussion about that before she finally accepted that I was taking her to the dentist, and dropping her off at Wuggerlands and 'no I'm not sure if you will be in time to do the tables'. Everything went quite well at the dentist and we were at Wuggerlands in good time. A lady came out of the office and we had an innocent little chat about this and that, and then she said something which she realised I knew nothing about.

'Oh yes' she said 'we thought Tina wasn't coming today as her taxi didn't arrive.'

Tina's taxi? I said a bit bemused.

Oh yes she said we usually see it arrive by 10.00 at the latest.

'He's a nice chap isn't he Tina?

I must say that Tina didn't know what to say she just muttered something like he's alright. And then she went off and I went to work as someone had been covering for me, giving us both time to think what to say to each other.

After Tina and I came home, separate ways of course, and after Neighbours had finished I approached the subject of the taxi trips.

"Don't you like going on the bus," I asked.

"Course I do" she replied.

"Well I wasn't sure why you had to get a taxi to Wuggerlands, did you miss the bus?"

"Not really, she said, but hadn't finished ma coffee, it didn't wait."

"Tina the bus has to get to all the stops that it has to make. it can't wait for you to finish your coffee, how many times have you taken a taxi and what about paying?"

"I don't know do I?"

"And paying" I repeated.

"Course I do" she said.

That's where all her money is going, I thought.

"Well Tina do you know that if you don't use your bus pass Val will have to take it from you and give it back to the council. "

"She won't" says Tina but I can see that she is thinking about that.

After East Enders had finished she came into the room, burst into tears and said, "sorry mum I'll go on the bus."

"That is a good idea Tina and can you make sure that you drink your coffee and go and wait in the queue. You know that those taxis are waiting to take a disabled person because they are not able to get on the bus. You can get on a bus can't you?"

"Course I can."

So that little episode ended quite happily. It wasn't the fact that she had taken to taxi riding, which would probably have come to an end, but without any evidence of wrong doing, Tina was a vulnerable lady and, I felt, safer travelling on the bus plus for the short time that she was on it, she could do her greeting and meeting. To my knowledge the taxi travelling was not repeated.

Fridays were looked forward to with pleasure by Tina because it was fish sandwich day! I don't know how this tradition started but we suddenly realised that she wasn't making her Friday lunch on Thursday evenings.

"He makes me a fish sandwich that's why."

By he I think she meant the cook. "Is that alright for him to do that Tina, you didn't ask did you."

"No I did not," she said with emphasis.

(Tina was really a pescatarian but because it was a difficult word to say because of her developing stammer, we stuck to referring to her diet as vegetarian.)

So back to the fish sandwich yes they were enjoyed every week until one Friday.... Grandson William, who was about 18 months in age, had stayed overnight and Tina had entertained him with her popping sounds and chatter, and the next day the plan was to pick up Tina from Wuggerlands, after her lunch of course, to take her with us returning William back to his mum and dad.

"We will pick you up at 2.00pm Tina, it will be nice to see Lou and Spen again won't it? So don't leave Wuggerlands will you Tina?"

She seemed quite acceptable to these arrangements but I thought that we should get their early just in case....We arrived and waited and waited. William was looking worried he wanted to get back to his mum and dad. I was on the point of getting out of the car when suddenly Tina appeared from the doorway with a thunderous look on her face!

"Are you alright Tina?"silly question, to which she replied,

"No 'am not, no fish sandwich. He's ran out."

Oh my goodness that has never happened before. Poor Tina.

"Haven't you had any lunch at all then Tina" I asked.

"No I've not. Not noffing."

"Oh dear well we'll stop at a shop on the way and see what they have. "

Tina is brightening up a bit now and is talking to William 'no lunch, ave had noffing.' William isn't following this but I think he was pleased that she looked happier. However more bad news no sandwiches left in the shop.

"Never mind Louise will have made some tea for us Tina, would you like a piece of apple to be going on with."

"No a do not."

She did get a very nice early tea from Lou, I think there were fish fingers and chips on offer. Quite appropriate I thought. The story of the non existent fish sandwich ran and ran. If there was a gap in conversation with people who knew Tina, I would ask if they would like to hear the fish sandwich story. Tina and I would tell it between us.

The days and weeks are passing quite quickly now. I am conscious of the passage of time as Tina came home one day and remarked that Pat was retiring. My stomach lurched when I heard this news as Pat was Tina's rock. It was she who had said that Tina must stay at Wuggerlands and not go to help out after lunch at the day centre because she had dropped a glass on the floor and picked up the broken glass with her bare hands. The lady in charge said that Tina could only come over if another helper came with her. I could see her point. So Tina stayed at Wuggerlands with Pat all through the staff dinner time and did some washing up there.

However it had given me a wake up call and I knew that I had to think of another place for her. Yes I could have consulted the professionals, but I had learnt that it is better to see them with a plan. I kept my eyes open. I used to attend various meetings in the room where the Monday club was held near the park view centre,and one meeting was about the Aspires project. The manager Jackie Murphy said that, 'Everybody can do something.' I liked her attitude and thought that Tina would fit in to this environment.

Watch out for developments folks.

RELIGION

If you asked Tina if she believed in God she would have replied in two ways, the off hand way,

"Not really", or the more thoughtful approach, "Grandma does".

Tina's thought processes seemed to be that if one member of her family either believed in something or pursued an interest, then that would be good enough for her. She need not concern herself with the subject of religion because in her reckoning that was grandma's department.

However, she has had moments of deep religiosity especially after her Grandma died. If we were visiting a church or cathedral, perhaps on holiday when Tina would be with us, she would head off up to the high altar and kneel down. There was usually an official person lurking around this area who may have liked to have moved Tina on but sensibly didn't attempt to do so. After a few moments of meditation Tina would rise to her feet and wander about until she had spotted us. She would then approach us in tears.

"Do you want to light a candle for grandma?"

"Yes I do."

It was always a relief to find candles and matches on the stand and the right amount of money in either mine or Tina's pocket. She much preferred it to be my pocket. The tears had gone, the candle was lit and we walked off to find whoever we were with. The routine had been adhered to and Tina left contented. We probably went for a drink as all that meditation can make you thirsty.

Thank God if there was a rail to assist her to kneel down without toppling over, as she had 'come a cropper' once in grandma's church at Thornhill Lees. Tina watched her grandma genuflect before getting into her churchwarden pew, and apparently tried to copy the procedure of going down on one knee, before getting into her designated pew. I heard a flurry of activity to the accompaniment of,

"Eeee a yourl rite love" spoken loudly.

I was busy organising Tina's younger sisters' seating arrangement for minimal level of disruption along the pew and Grandma had already gone into church mode and was kneeling saying her prayers. Members of the congregation who had been watching this attempt at genuflecting swiftly came to her aid and, the ladies who always thought Tina's actions a welcome distraction had rushed over to help her up, and carefully place her at the end of the pew. NO that wouldn't do! Tina would be making a bolt out if she got bored, probably after 5 minutes. Dignified sister was moved to the end, which triggered off wailing from the undignified sister. All this commotion annoyed my mum as churches were for praying in and even her granddaughters, who she dearly loved, would not be forgiven for encouraging the congregation to start a discussion on Tina's problems,

"Ah poor kid she can't elp it y'naw."

"A naw, but she dus well when ya think o them uthers!"

Yorkshire ladies always seem to speak in a grim tone when referring to a doom and gloom issue, this time disability, think of Last of the Summer Wine and the ladies at their tea parties spreading their misgivings.

Tina was baptized on the 2nd December 1958 in Thornhill Lees church where incidently her mum and dad were married. It was her grandma's birthday a nice little coincidence. It was a quiet affair as the mum wasn't in the loop yet of knowing she had a mentally handicapped child and 'best not to attract too much attention' I could imagine the interlopers thinking. Yes a quiet affair with the families and the god parents. But we did go into 'the room', the one in the house designated for special events, for our little tea afterwards. That was Tina's initiation into the Christian life.

She was confirmed with the dignified sister at North Wootton church. They attended the confirmation classes together. Thank you dignified sister (Rachel). I can only guess at Tina's demeanour during these sessions as Rachel was very stoical and I can't remember her coming home and exploding as to Tina's incorrect behaviour. I just hope she didn't sit picking her nose!

At the actual confirmation I can just remember Tina not kneeling down when the bishop needed to put his hand on her head. Rachel after a couple of tugs on Tina's arm gave up and Tina remained standing during the procedure. The Bishop having to lift his arm up somewhat. I can imagine if I had said to her,

"Tina why didn't you kneel down?" she would reply,

"I couldn't that's why" and of course there wasn't a rail to help her.

The Holy Communion service must have followed and I am presuming Tina managed wafer and wine with satisfaction, or I can't remember anything negative being said about the situation. Tea and biscuits followed, the icing on the cake of confirmation.

I am not going to pontificate on whether it was correct for someone to take on a sacrament without the full depth of understanding of it all. Do many of us really? It was a rite of passage to a sharing of the last supper, from which I could not see any reason for Tina to be excluded. Fortunately the vicar was in agreement so this did not turn into a battle. Anyway if we are going down the religious route and we are all created in God's image!? Then enough said.

When Tina was 21 she was asked if she would like to go on a pilgrimage to Lourdes. Tina always the eager beaver to go on a jolly said 'yes definitely'.

The Roman Catholic church took a group of children with a disability away every year and although Tina at 21 was a bit out of this age range they had decided to include her. The primary reason for a pilgrimage to Lourdes was to ask for healing of your affliction but as one of the organisers said, in a matter of fact way, that it would be a very nice holiday if nothing else happened. I didn't bother telling Tina it was to 'heal her affliction'.

She returned, still Tina, complete with a sweat shirt with 'Lourdes' emblazoned over the front. I think there was a small bottle of holy water for Grandma and I know that there was a boy friend called Karl who lived quite near and would start to visit regularly. He would appear quietly,

"Came on the bus", Karl was a young man of few words, so in answer to,

"Does mum or dad know you are here?"

“Yes”. That one word would suffice.

Sometimes they did not as Karl was a secretive character who liked his independence and would make up his mind on the spur of the moment. He was used to the buses as was Tina and loved the freedom to come and go as he pleased. Karl would ask if Tina could go over for a Sunday lunch,

‘Yes definitely’ would be the reply. On the day of the lunch Karl might stay in, he might not. If something more interesting had turned up he would be out. Tina didn’t mind as she was very fond of his mum.

Tina went on another pilgrimage to Israel. This time with myself, Sheila, the friend from the St Edmundsbury road chapter, auntie Audrey (A1) her godmother and uncle Alan (A2) who in his ministerial position was the leader of the gang, I mean group. They belonged to the charismatic wing of the United Reformed church.

Tina enjoyed the services at his church as the hymns were accompanied with clapping. It was people friendly and members of the congregation could stand at the front and ask either for God’s blessing for someone in a bad situation, or to invite everyone to share their joy at a miracle which had taken place. It could be very moving listening to all the stories, it could also be very long. So Tina would have to make at least two trips to the toilet.

Tina could join in quite happily with clapping and actually learned a couple of choruses “If you’re happy and you know it clap your hands” and “I’m inright outright upright downright” etc, something tangible for Tina to do.

So, back to the pilgrimage, when we were trying to switch the guide off on the bus we all started to clap and sing before we went to sleep one by one, and the guide was left talking to himself.

Tina, as always, milked the situation and got on well with everyone except perhaps the guide who could not understand why she needed the toilet 4 hours after travelling! everyone else needed the toilet too but nobody dared to say. Tina and I on one occasion skived off for a longer toilet stop than was permitted, and returned to find the guide waiting for us before he started another lengthy spiel, and the rest of the poor folks desperately still needing the toilet!

At this stop was a beach and Tina was so desperate to paddle, and so after the pleading of "go on mum" I couldn't stop myself and Tina and I went into the water and the rest followed. We were all like children screeching and whooping for at least 15 minutes and then we had to try and get dry and return to the bus. The driver was not happy and said that we would have to miss out a church and we all cheered quietly and tried to look attentive for the rest of the journey back to the hotel.

The plus of the holiday for Tina was the company, the food and the attention especially being presented with a huge birthday cake festooned with candles I think she was 31.

The boat trip on the sea of Galilee was so quietly moving, a real change from the bustling land sights even Tina looked relaxed and peaceful until she suddenly said,

"Shall I jump in?" That dragged me out of my reverie and we all shouted 'no Tina' and she laughed. I think our escort was on the point of a nervous breakdown. I hope the tip was enough to compensate for his stress.

The sights and the commentary were too complicated for most of us, so we let most of what we were told float over our heads, including Tina's, who cheered up whenever we moved off. Outside the city of Jerusalem she took a nice picture of me with "the dome on the rock" in the background.

And the icing on the cake of the pilgrimage was we were able to persuade our leader to take us to a show, as Tina could not possibly be on holiday/pilgrimage without going to a show!

Back to the act of communion and Tina's approach to it. For folks who are not familiar with this procedure; the plan is to come out of your pew and quietly in a line wander up to the altar kneel down receive the wafer and wine and then return to your pew in a way befitting what you have just received and mindful that other people are still waiting.

Tina had a slightly different agenda depending on what mood she was in on the day. She was not British when it came to queuing so she would veer slightly outwards, walk on the outside of the queue going forwards, if folks had started to return it got a little tricky and bumpy.

"Oh sorry" someone would whisper,

"T's alright" Tina would reply never admitting that it was her fault, and then tuck back into perhaps one in front of me just to see if it worked. It usually did so she got bolder, three or four next time, and unless someone was so deep in thought/prayer she tucked in again, if they were so deep in thought or prayer there may be a collision, for which not Tina, but the one in thought or prayer was apologetic!

Now Tina is way in front of me and in a different place or with a different vicar there may be a doubt as to 'can Tina receive the wafer and wine'. Pity the poor vicar on that day, so I have to step out of line tuck in behind her and help the vicar/Tina out. Even though she would have held out her hands in the correct position I could sense some vicars were a bit nervous. The vicar would still be holding the host/wafer up high, either wondering what on earth to do with it or praying for guidance……it may have been on the point of wobbling and Tina may have been on the point of making a grab for it. Could she or couldn't she the pause said? Look at me vicar I'm nodding my head! And the vicar would finally twig, and Tina would get her wafer.

We are not Roman Catholic where the wafer is put into the mouth or the poor vicar may have been missing his hand. And what a good job that the cup was held by the celebrant as Tina never understood 'sip'. The cup would have been drained by Tina's slurp and more wine would have had to be consecrated. Does not bear thinking about.

If Tina was not in the best of temperament she would say she would come up to the altar, and then return to our pew, or one belonging to someone else, after a few steps. When I returned she would be in floods of tears, but I didn't have much sympathy.

"Why did you go back Tina?"

"I've got a pain that's why", so I was left feeling wicked.

Tina sometimes would be in gung-ho mode and decide that she would be doing "it" all by herself,

"In the correct way Tina" I would hiss "keep next to me".

Yes everything went well and then I thought we should return to the pew. No movement from Tina.

"Come on Tina" I would try and whisper but Tina was having none of it and then the dreaded,

"Not yet". I just knew I had to leave her to it and I got up and started my return, praying madly that she would follow and she usually did as she had said, she was 'doing it herself 'and why not.

One quick story before we leave this chapter. The eternal triangle of Tony, Tina and me, had gone on a weekend bus trip to London, then to fireworks at Leeds Castle, very exciting. We went on the London Eye the day we arrived. Tina loved the eye for 2 reasons, she loved heights and she knew I did not. We ascended so slowly, Tina jeering at me all the time and "are you nervous" she kept shouting so definitely the people in our pod would be aware of my fear as maybe the rest of the riders. We grounded safely and carried on to our destination, Tina carrying a picture of herself in the pod.

We all enjoyed the fireworks at Leeds Castle and at the same venue West Life were playing as we could hear strains of their music coming through the pauses in the whizzes and bangs. Tina remarked that her friend Wendy would have "liked that". Tina did have a kind nature but was not that keen on West Life.

The next day we were taken to Greenwich and saw the Cutty Sark,

"Look Tina there's the Cutty Sark."

"It's a boat" replied Tina who had the knack of downgrading works of wonder. We remained for a short while, Tony being completely besotted with it.

"He's obsessed"! remarked Tina who after giving it the quick once over was eager to move on.

Up to the observatory, it was interesting to see the picture of Tina with one foot on either side of the dateline. Walked up the steps inside and then down the hill to the chapel.

"Shall we go in" said I, Tony and Tina non committal. Tina immediately started to look for a candle to light. Suddenly we realised that there was going to be a service! Shock horror in a strange church with an atheist and Tina who was beginning to be passing her sell by date - meaning she is fed up and we must get going. Too late, the procession of officiate, choir and helpers/altar boys is coming up those treacherous steps. So how could we escape?

"Will we be in time for the bus?" I ask Tony (who doesn't want to be there) he nods and looks resigned, relay this to Tina.

"We have to wait here for the bus.

"What here" incredulous tone from Tina studying her watch.

The service starts and I despair and say to Tony (who doesn't want to be there) it's a sung communion service, it will be very nice but might be longer than 1 hour! Tony's head drops and Tina doesn't look best pleased. The service is running it's course and Tony (who doesn't want to be there) is at least standing and sitting in the right places. Tina is doing her own thing of just before we sit down Tina stands up and remains standing when everyone is seated. Very difficult for Tina, who could not understand the words or say the prayers, ask forgiveness for her sins 'that's stupid that is'. She might have even said 'like what'. We have passed the sermon and are approaching the consecration, why I asked Tina if she was coming up to the altar I am not sure, anyway Tina shook her head so I relayed that to Tony,

"Tina's stopping here!"

Oh no she didn't! Is it pantomime time now because I had walked a few paces when Tina as predictably had changed her mind and caught me up saying,

"I'm here" in an audible voice.

After that the operation went smoothly, there was a rail to lean on in a slight semi circle, I nodded to the vicar, Tina received communion and we left the altar together BUT half way back to the pew poor Tina just burst into loud sobs, Tony gathered up all our belongings and we left to hang about outside in the gloom. Tina hadn't lit her candle, but as it was the end of the service I took Tina back in, Tony remaining outside and probably wishing the ground would open up as he is a private person.

However he was asked if the young lady was all right and Tina was asked the same whilst we were lighting the candle.*

After that we were back on the bus and homeward bound. Tina telling "the bus" that she had cried in church, and as the Chinese whisper of the event circulated it had acquired different strands to the story. So as I walked to our seats which was taking a long time, I said 'no she wasn't ill/ hadn't fainted or fallen/ didn't need the toilet (that was a first) she just wanted to light a candle in memory of her grandma.' And the bus erupted with sighs of sympathy, and I could collapse in the seat on my own as the story had been finalised and Tina had snuggled up to Tony.

As the folks alighted from the bus they all shouted their goodbyes to Tina. And she had only known them for a weekend.

What would they tell their friends and family, I can hear it now.

'We met this young girl with her mum and dad....no that weren't her dad 'cos she said Tone; oh I di'nt hear that; no I keep saying you should hev yore hairing aid in; well we met this girl Tiner and she'd got herself upset in that there chapel cos she wanted to pay her respects to her nan wot hed died but there weren't no where to do it; well that wor a shame and she were a nice girl with that downs business; oh she wor retarded then? She were but she wor enjoying hersel an it dint stop wot she did. It were just sad about that candle thing; was they religious then; they must a bin else they wunt be in that there chapel.'

* Whenever the best mate and I travel, we usually head for a church and light a candle as Tina would have wanted.

Now she has joined the musicians for the evening

15

Changes

Pat's decision to retire from Wuggerlands left me with a decision that I would have to make.

We have spoken of the broken glasses incident, an accident that could happen to anyone, but there were two other incidents that I could not ignore.

In the bus station one evening Tina followed two girls who lived near to us onto the wrong bus, they were going elsewhere and kindly phoned their mother to say that Tina was on the bus and could she let us know. Then we had a phone call from an upset Tina not knowing where she was going. A young lady passenger spoke to me on Tina's phone to say that the bus was going to Hunstanton and she was getting off in Dersingham. The young lady had spoken to the driver and he said he would make sure that she stayed on the bus until they had reached the destination of Hunstanton. It was my day of grandma duties with seven months old Claire so Tony was going to pick up Tina.

I spoke to the young lady on Tina's phone as she did not want to leave without knowing that someone would be there when the bus arrived. The bus driver waited until Tony arrived, he had asked Tina if she would like to remain sitting on the bus until she was picked up as it was the last trip of his shift, giving him the time to wait.

Tina burst into tears with relief when she finally got into the car and they made their way home.

There are some people who will go the final mile to help someone. The two girls who told their mum, the young lady on the bus and the bus driver. Many years later, but a big thank you to them all.

The third incident was in the kitchen at Wuggerlands. Tina had been asked to put something on the draining board, which she must have done many times, only this time she could not find it. She might have been getting tired or waiting to leave. One can always think of many reasons/ excuses why some things happen but when incidents build up you cannot turn a blind eye. Setting the tables was also becoming a problem, I think someone else was setting them for her. I did not want Tina to remain at Wuggerlands and then be asked to leave, it is better to go before you are pushed. We are strongly considering it.

One day I was at a meeting of the Parent/Carer group. The chairman was sharing some information with us concerning the psychotherapist group at Park View. Surprisingly I had never met them before, well not really surprising as Tina had not had a psychological problem. We were informed that this team would be pleased to listen to any problems parents were having with regard to behaviour, mood change, forgetfulness indeed anything which was against their norm.

So I made an appointment and was seen by Stella and Phil. They had come prepared with their pads and pens.

I explained about the signs of difference in Tina's behaviour:

Not dancing (she used to love it), sitting down at the first opportunity.

Isolating herself more. She was always so gregarious.

Losing/ misplacing hats, gloves, her bus pass and purse. The bus company were so kind and even started to recognise my voice when I enquired about them.

The upshot was that Phil would take Tina's case and an appointment was made for him to come and do a base line assessment. Tina enjoyed this and she ended with a very low score. This disappointed her as she wanted a high one! This was repeated 4 months later, still good. Now we had a breathing space, we had to inform Phil if things deteriorated.

During this period of calm we had two lots of exciting news; both of Tina's sisters were pregnant, first Louise and then Rachel. We thought it a good idea if Tina knitted a blanket for each baby, she did enjoy knitting, as long as someone was on hand to pick up the stitches. The squares were finished and dear Sheila, remember the 'ask a busy woman', volunteered to crochet them together.

The babies duly arrived, a heavy weight 9lb 5oz William Oliver Terence (Will) caesarean birth 2 weeks late, his blanket had been completed. Tina was taken by Grandma and a heavily pregnant auntie Rachel to see her 'lickle' nephew, my grandson, Tina was passing on the news to all she met that she was now an aunt.

Nine days after Will being born, I managed to persuade Rachel to come out of the swimming baths as she had been having twinges and I thought she needed to go to the hospital. Plus it would be an inconvenience if the pool had to be drained following the birth of her baby. Things were happening and two or thee days later, after an appointment as an out patient, she was admitted onto the ward. Rachel was ensconced in the hospital, John, dad to be, was wandering about in the hospital and I was in a dilemma because I had offered to take Sheila to the Norwich hospital for one of her numerous appointments. Would I be needed, 'no' said both John and Rachel, 'you take Sheila.'

Tina had mentioned about 'going to see her sister', so it must have been a Wuggerlands day and she knew that the bus she had caught from the bus station stopped at the hospital! Was she fobbed off by me, by saying that we would all go later on when the baby had been born? I should have realised......oh well. As Sheila left the hospital I had both Rachel and Tina on my mind, at least I knew where Rachel was, hopefully in capable hands, but Tina, what was she doing? I didn't have to wait long to find out.

We were on the A47, the phone rang and Sheila picked it up'

"Hello Tina are you alright."

"Course I am, where's mum. I want her."

"She's driving Tina, she can't talk on the phone."

"Ask her where she is," says me.

"Tina where are you," pause, "what, at the hospital?"

"Tell her to have a coffee and wait for us."

Off we went again, the traffic queue was horrendous down Gayton Rd so we had to abandon Sheila as near as we could get her to her daughter's house and back track to the hospital.

As you go into the hospital you are almost in the café, and there on a chair all on her own was a sad looking Tina, what a relief! The whole story came out in bits and pieces over the next few weeks, everyone involved adding their piece of information, I even met one of the midwives, somewhere.

But what was happening on the ward has the star of the show arrived yet? We didn't have long to wait. John suddenly appeared with a huge grin on his face and looking straight at Tina said,

"What is it Tina," and she said,

"A Girl"

"Yes" said John, and Tina cheered and clapped and we were all very relieved. Mum and baby were fine, and that is the day Claire Elizabeth came into our lives, joining Will in the middle of my heart.

I was amazed that Tina found her way to the maternity department, John said the door opened and in came Tina with a nurse escort, remember this was a sterile area as Rachel was waiting to have a Ceasarian section! John told Tina to go back downstairs and ring 'your mum' and tell me where she was. That was the phone call into my car as we were on the A47.

Sometimes I just cannot put myself into Tina's shoes and have an explanation for what she has just done, this time I could. I think she wanted to show some solidarity with her sister as a thank you for looking after her at the monthly discos at North Wootton village hall, the Saturday morning cinema when invariably Tina needed the toilet half way through, the attempted borrowing of one of her bags, a regular occurrence, and sneaking off to the ATC with Rachel's new Drifters record. Yes that's right - the one that arrived back with a bite out of it. Yes this was Tina wanting to make amends and show her sister some support. One thing that Tina could do was finish Claire's blanket. She was three weeks early, and the nurses thought that Rachel was hallucinating as she kept saying that the baby could not come yet because the blanket wasn't ready.

I cannot move away from these births without mentioning Edward Peter, Claire's brother and nearly 2 years younger than her. The evening after he was born I took Claire who had been staying with us and Tina to see the new arrival. His mum and dad looked shattered and he looked quite solitary in his cot on the other side of the room. That was when I fell 'in love' with him. Sadly Tina just couldn't finish his blanket and so dear Sheila came to the rescue and attempted to finish it in Tina's style. Ask that busy woman again!

During this time I attended a workshop experiencing what it is like for someone with dementia to do simple tasks, and it came as a God send. First we had to put on a pair of very thick gloves and then try and pick up a pencil and write our name. We all found this extremely difficult and the names were unreadable. It was a relief to get rid of the gloves, but someone with dementia is not wearing gloves, they have hands which don't function as they did before. Cutting up food and then putting the fork or spoon to your mouth is also difficult and may necessitate having to wear something around your neck, I don't like to use the word - bib.

What about going to the toilet and not be able to clean yourself up? If you are in your own home and you emerge from the toilet with disarranged clothes, someone will assist you. Not so easy when a toilet break is needed during a shopping trip. I was always pleased when Tina and I could fit into a toilet, and I would have to persuade her to 'Just wait Tina' until I had 'been', and we could both exit the toilet with our clothing suitably arranged. I am thinking of the aircraft travel now, we carried on travelling with Tina as long as was possible.

The speaker was Jackie, who ran Aspires the project I had been interested in, which was a workshop/ a cottage industry she had developed in Fincham Norfolk. Clients gave her orders for small part assemblies suitable for adults with learning disabilities which, with guidance, they were able to perform. And that is where the phrase 'Everybody can do something' came from.

I was sold! That sounded perfect. At the end of the meeting I asked if I could come and see for myself as to whether it would suit Tina. The place had a very warm feeling about it. I did know some of the people, and I was sure that there would be something that she could do, so I arranged for Tina to see for herself.

I would have to replan Tina's life, which would mean giving up Wuggerlands, without Pat she wouldn't cope, and, as I have always thought, better to go before one is pushed. But….. the buses, coffee stops, bags of crisps, the chats to all and sundry, play group and Wuggerlands with the Friday fish sandwich…what am I doing? I felt wretched. I started to think of all the differences that had been happening to Tina, hoping it would give me the confidence to do the right thing!

'Well come on Josette,' I thought, 'her life isn't going to stand still waiting for you to make up your mind, go with what you think will be right for her and take her to look.' I did not need to have been anxious, we walked in to a hail of 'hello Tina, are you coming to work with us',and giggling and saying in a jokey way that, 'Oh no look who's coming' and Tina replying with a smile 'shurrup you.'Yes I could see that it was going to work out. She sat down on a vacant chair.

Jackie started talking to me and giving me some details which I would have to sign on behalf of Tina, mostly to do with her health. Then she talked to Tina asking her questions as to what did she like doing? What did she like to eat?* Who did she know here? The group was made up of members from the Monday night club or The Befrienders, who Tina knew, but there were some who she had never seen before - so more people to add to her list for details of their lives. The people who knew her very well started to answer all the questions which gave Tina the time to observe who was there, and see if anyone had a bag of crisps open. Then a very jolly lady by the name of Sandra came to talk to her and that is how Sandra came into Tina's life, taking over from Pat, but we are not quite there yet. The leaving party from Wuggerlands had to be arranged.

Lots of people came to witness this event. It was happy and sad in equal measures, 28 years is a long time in anyones' work life and Tina ,as always,

---

* She could say with pride that she was a vegetarian, so when the group went to a local pub around Christmas time for a meal, Tina would have the veggie alternative. She never faltered from her steadfast belief in vegetarianism.

had certainly made her mark at Wuggerlands, or now that Tina is leaving this behind, perhaps we should begin to say Woodlands.

Towards the end of the celebrations I saw Tina walk to look in the kitchen door, walk away, and then burst into tears. It was to be expected. When she had recovered she started her rounds to say her goodbyes'. There were more tears from the staff and residents and finally we left with the promise that she would come to Pat's leaving party.

I would like to print 'Congratulations' from a newsletter of West Norfolk Mencap. This is exactly what was written:-

'There were tears and smiles, champagne and cake recently when Tina Swann retired from her role as dining room assistant at Woodlands Home for the Elderly. Tina had been volunteering there for an amazing 28 years and staff and residents were sorry to see her go. But everyone wished her well for the future.'

There is a picture of Tina, with Pat's help, cutting the cake, watched over by the manager.

So another chapter in Tina's life would soon begin.

The period of calm which had lasted for 16 months was at an end now as Tina's scores were rising, it seemed rapidly, and because Phil wanted to eliminate all the physical reasons, an appointment was made with the private consultant to see if her heart, which had a hole from birth, would cope with an anaesthetic for a cataract removal. Tina had been to see an optician in Dersingham, a very thorough person who diagnosed a cataract which was overlapping her short and her long vision. It was a nasty problem that would affect her sight immensely, poor Tina, thank goodness he was thorough and kind to her.

So one Saturday morning, Tina (with Mum and Tone) went to the private hospital, to see Mr ?. A charming man, who treated Tina with kindness and respect. (I don't think she asked him for his CV.) He was satisfied with her heart condition, so she was ready to have the cataract removed.

Sorry folks but this meeting will have to pop in here. We were on the Scottish border at a wedding of one of Marie and Jim's boys. At the meal

Tina was sitting next to a beef farmer, we knew that as he had introduced himself to her and told her what work he did, actually he looked very much like David Cameron the politician, who was the apple of Tina's eye.

Beef was on the menu and when Tina realised this she, speaking loudly, told almost the whole room that she didn't eat meat as she was vegetarian. Even adding her one liner of 'You shouldn't kill animals for food.' Well Tony and I were nearly under the table as in 'when or where can we go'!

We shouldn't have worried as 'David' seemed very impressed with Tina speaking up for her principles. Before the end of what had been a very interesting day, Tina, who had danced with her 'friend', managed to persuade Marie to sing the banned song, although it was done quietly. The whiskey helped.

Louise and Spencer's Wedding

This wedding seemed to be a long time coming.

At first it was going to be a small, rather plain affair, no fuss, Louise wasn't even having a special dress! Gradually over the days, months and eventually years, the changes came and went, and during this time William was born so we were on the change again. Tina meanwhile was getting used to being an auntie, she had to of course as Claire was born 11 days later. Tina was thrilled with these two new additions which took her focus off the wedding plans. In fact she may have forgotten about the whole thing as year followed year and another new addition called Edward was born, a brother for Claire.

Finally in 2006 the day was booked at the registrar office and Tina was going to give Louise away.

The dad had died in 1994 and so Louise thought it would be nice for Tina to have that role. Some people were surprised at Louise's choice but she stuck with it as she wanted Tina to have a main part in her wedding as she had in Rachel's; however time has moved on and Tina is becoming more needy because dementia does not take a break and trips to the toilet were becoming more intense.

So let us keep hoping that she will be fine on the day. She was going to wear a lovely outfit as Louise had finally decided to wear a white long dress, in short a wedding dress.

Tina was wearing a pale green skirt which was softly flowing to just above her ankles and a paler green short jacket with a nipped in waist. A pair of white pump type shoes completed the outfit. Again she looked very smart, but this time at this occasion she seemed unaware of what was happening and she did need support during the whole procedure.

Then it was photograph time, no confetti this time, the pictures were lovely and then we were off to the party, with speeches of course. The weather was sunny and warm, lovely for relaxing although Tina, with me in tow, spent a long time in the toilet. Fortunately Louise and Spencer had decided to have the reception in their garden with a climbing frame for the children, so everyone was content and it was relaxing for me knowing that the toilet was always near for Tina.

Well both Tina's sisters are married now, a friend had asked me if Tina was envious of them and I could say quite honestly that no she, at this stage of her life, was becoming more insular. Her mind and her body were changing, her world was becoming more self absorbed.

Retirement – Tina is looking at her card. The young lady brought another cake from Crossroads where Tina had also worked.

Tracy, Tina and Josette at Norton Hill miniature train ride fundraiser.

Enjoying a train ride at Norton Hill, Snettisham. Rachel, Josette's back and Tina's front showing her eye dressing.

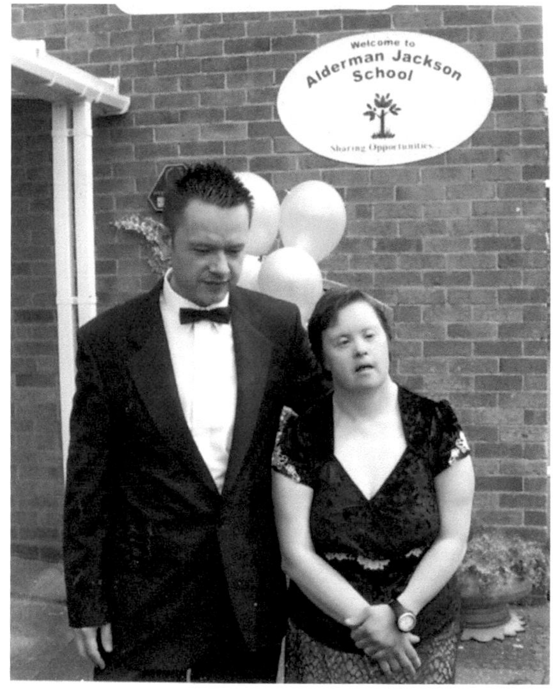

Tina with her hero Spikey Mike from Tom Thumb after the presentation.

Tina, looking very smart, looks to be receiving a gift from the manager at the play group with the children watching on.

Tina with the beef farmer – read the story.

16

Decisions

Tina seems to be settling in at Aspires very well, I didn't think it would be difficult as in the past she had readily adapted to all the changes of schools, houses, even different towns, were taken in her stride. But she was old Tina then, and now she has to drag along the being that is making its presence felt in her brain - dementia. I have to get used to saying that word now because it is there, a part of Tina, and having so much more impact than the word 'Down's', and causing so much more damage.

So she is new Tina now. Some days she will be happy and cheerful and if it is an Aspires day will be ready and on time for her taxi. Yes she is being transported again, I am rather upset by this but Tina does not appear to be, so again I have to live with that. Yes they were the good days and, we were still getting our morning tea – with bags out!

Sadly she did have bad days, mostly they were the build up to a seizure, e.g pains in her tummy which usually meant she needed the toilet. She was taking Donepezil now to try and alleviate the seizures, 10mg then reduced to 5mg, which did help the bowel situation.

To give 'the best mate' and myself some respite and to prepare, I suppose for Tina eventually moving to some form of care, (notice at the moment I am using the C word without the prefix of UN and I don't mean the united nations), it was decided to introduce Tina to Urvi, a very pleasant lady, who was in charge of about four people with learning disabilities who could manage a daily routine for themselves and some appropriate house care with added help. They lived in a small bungalow in Swaffham. Tina was taken out with the carer twice a week for a few hours but soon got bored with that arrangement, and we did not think that it was a sufficient enough for her to experience the reality living apart from us. We shall see!

I will fall back on remembering what my good friend Helen said,

"If it doesn't suit you and Tony (best mate) and if Tina is unhappy you can always bring her back."

We had also looked at a house to share in North Lynn, but I thought the rooms would be too small for Tina, she did like to roam around and this would have curtailed her movements, so we did say no to that offer. I bitterly regretted that decision as I will explain as this story develops.

So the time has come now for us to look at the uncare home in ? St James across the border in Lincolnshire near to the town of Wisbech. How I came to hate that place. But it was made to sound doable and reasonable, Tina would still go to Aspires by taxi and most weekends she would be brought to stay with us.

17

Tina leaves home

We went to visit the care home prior to Tina leaving our home and all seemed to be well. We were greeted by the manager who walked towards us drying her hands. I think she had been baking. Suddenly I felt Tina taking hold of my hand, this was very rare for Tina. She was never phased with new situations, she would have gone into question time. you know, are you married, what's his name, kids, age etc. There was nothing, she just stood as if rooted to the spot. This did not auger well, even with the onset of dementia I was expecting her to say 'what's your name'.

I would have to speak to the social worker about this. We arrived back home and Tina went into her room.

Tony, after hearing of Tina's attitude, blunt as usual just said

"Well she'll have to stay here, I said she wouldn't like it. She'll stay with us, we can manage. This is her home."

I was agreeing with him but looking ahead without support I knew it would not be possible. We needed carers and for that we would need council money to support this need.

"Let us see how things go," I suggested to Tony.

He wasn't happy about that, well neither was I, but I felt we must try Tina there and if it wasn't working for her, then remembering Helen's wise advice, that would be ammunition to bring her back.

Tina is now in residence in the uncare home, with plenty of visits by us, sometimes together, sometimes Tony going in the night time.

"I knew you were worried about her so I went to see if she was asleep." He said.

Louise would see Will off to school and then go over to the Hollow to see what was happening, also to take things for Tina which had been just 'forgotten', pads which were delivered to the home usually ran out before the next delivery. Another item which Tina could not do without now was thickener, which was, or should have been, used for all her drinks and some of her food. She could choke if she was poorly fed or given a drink too quickly. She now had the label of Dysphagia.

I wasn't seeing much organisation into the way that items were ordered for Tina from the surgery. When they had run out of thickener, why was it was left to us to replace? Surely that can't be right? Also we had to check Tina's doctors appointments and tell them if we had found sore places on her skin.

A young lady who Tina had known for a long time, school, college, gateway club, usual places, although not a good friend of Tina's, was now living in the same house. One morning we had arrived to see Tina and she was sitting in the lounge area with this young lady. When I called out a greeting, Tina turned and looked at me and I was horrified to see that the side of her face was red and swollen.

"What have you done Tina, who has done that to you?"

Then one of the carers came from the kitchen and said that it was the young lady. I was very angry with the carer for leaving them together in the same room unsupervised with Tina, who for some reason 'the young lady' had turned against.

We carried on visiting Tina in our usual way, concentrating on Tina's bowel action, and what she was eating. Before Tina moved into the uncare home, we had a visit from a dietitian who very precisely had recorded all Tina's dietary requirements emphasising Tina's vegetarian diet. Junk type of snacks were not good for her so fresh food and protein in other forms were necessary to counteract the lack of meat and fish. The manager of the uncare home had also attended this food discussion which I thought a good idea, however one day after we had taken Tina out in the van she came back to a fish paste sandwich for her main meal!

What was the point I thought to myself? On the table, where they all ate together, was a very flashy menu, which I think only came out when visitors came.

Louise had seen recorded on Tina's notes that she was only having two meals a day.

I wanted her to have just one sachet of Movocol per day. If too much was given then there are excessive results, and she was extremely uncomfortable. I feel that sometimes the staff had no idea what we were talking about. I do not think that any training was given to them at all and they were just muddling through. A relief Polish nurse was sometimes on duty and she seemed to really understand what she was there for, ie the patients welfare. So she would chat with them all, even the man who stayed in his room, probably he thought that there was nothing to get up for, joined in the conversations. However this did not last very long and when I asked where she was I was told that she was not asked to return because one of the patients could not understand her. Her English was spoken very clearly, I think she was a threat to the manager. It was so depressing.

Where was the training? Who has employed these people who just think that they have to feed, perhaps toilet if they must, and turn the television on for entertainment? I was coming to the end of my ability to try and work with them. Tony was right!

It is very difficult for me to write this in a dispassionate way because even though this happened many years ago it is still raw.

So we will move on, we have now made the decision to bring Tina back to us, we had consulted the social workers who advised us not to mention our plans to the uncare home. I think that is referred to as 'hedging your bets', in short keep your plans to yourself.

This is rather strange, but Tina's body seemed to be taking control of the situation, by having two seizures in quick succession, the second one being a tonic clonic one. She was taken to A and E by two of the carers, who then left after Rachel and I had arrived at the hospital. Tina was taken to the Medical Assessment Unit after her blood tests for further investigation, and I, as usual, was going to stay with her..... of course. The powers that be in the care system did not want Tina on a 1to1 scheme as someone from the home would have had to stay with her, and deep down I was pleased because I would have stayed whatever.

A huge source of frustration over the next 2 days to me was that we were not allowed to have Tina's medication as they said it needed to be put on the data base. Could the doctors surgery not have been asked for this? For nearly two days Tina did not have Sodium Valproate, which was to prevent or lessen seizures and she is in hospital because of seizures. It was being reviewed!

So I spent the night with Tina in a side ward, in a not very comfy chair. She did sleep very well, just waking at about 3am. I think it was a seizure as her body was jerky and her eyes open and fixed. But at least we were near to each other and I felt comforted. Later two of the staff from the home came, Rachel came for me and took me home.

Rachel saw Tina at twelve midday, Tony took me at five pm ready for the evening shift. Tina had been given a super bed which in rotation moved her position and she seemed very happy. I was given a bowl of cornflakes, very welcome as I had not eaten much, just finishing Tina's scraps. Surely I must have fed Tina some breakfast, remember the dysphagia, and I must have had something before the 'night shift'. Bit muddly.

Our home was beginning to be inspected, initially to see if we would be able to make all the alterations needed before Tina could come back, for....well forever. I could understand this scrutiny but we were solid in what we intended to do. So where was Tina going to be placed.... in our bungalow? All of our rooms were too small to have a bed, wheelchair, or shower, so that is when 'The Hut' was transformed to perform its most useful function. It had been originally a garage, then turned into a games room, with Tony's beloved pool table in pride of place, but that would have to go. Tina had enjoyed many a game on it with some of the family and with Wendy when she came visiting with her mum, remember the badminton (?) I think Tina and Wendy were more equal partners on the snooker table.

But we are at this stage of Tina's life now, and Tony and I are committed to turning this space into what will be known as 'Tina's Hut'. We are funding all the alterations ourselves, it will be costly monetary wise, but it will be bringing Tina back to us and so, with help with her care, she will be near to us. That was our plan.

Tony would often say 'she's nothing to do with me' but we all knew how he doted on her and that her comfort and welfare came before a pool table. He had devoted himself to Tina, she had opened up his eyes and his heart to people with disabilities as he would often say, 'I've never met anyone like that before.'

They would often disagree, particularly about television programmes but it was good for both of them to have their own opinions. 'What about your opinions?', I hear you say, I kept out of it. They would 'debate' the stories in East Enders, you know Tina must never miss an instalment, so a short reply to Tony's teasing was usually 'Don't be daft Tone.'

Because Tina hated missing East Enders, on Monday evenings, (Gateway Club night) Tony was commissioned to record it, and he would be in serious trouble if he 'forgot', which he often did after either falling asleep or watching a cowboy.

A story of Tina's revenge....

On one April Fool's day Tina, as usual, came into our bedroom with the cups of tea and quietly said,

"Tone your factory's on fire!"

Well that did it! Tony was trying to leap out of bed, Tina was looking worried, and I thought that she must have heard it on the morning news, did she? Well then it suddenly clicked,

"Tina," I said "is that an April Fool joke?"

"Course it is," but she still looked worried.

"Oh Tony" said I, "Tina's April Fooled you."

However Tony could not wait to get to his beloved factory just to make sure it was still there.

We have always referred to that day as Happy Tuesday as it was easier for Tina to pronounce.

After that short divergence, (I was very impressed with how Tina had pulled off her joke,) we must concentrate on Tina's welfare whilst she is still in the uncare home.

Happier news from the council, 'an angel' of a lady is going to look into what funding we could have from them and that they do fund hoists. However we had a long, long way to go to get The Hut into the condition which passed all the hoops it will needed to get through.

We had already had a price of £2,000 for the drains because there had never been a toilet in The Hut, and we were not on main drains then. Although Tina would not need to use the toilet, the carers would, and Tina would be needing a shower with a chair as she now could not stand, and a huge wet room to allow two carers, or one including me, to be in the room as well.

The trench had to be dug out from the side of the hut across what will be the car parking area to the side of our house, and meet up with the drain already in situ. Two cheerful young men were the diggers and they both recognised me from the school where I worked as they were pupils at the time. So we got off to a good start. And the kettle went on!

Back to Tina's situation.

We have just had the good news from Helen to say that Mandy from Mencap, a very capable woman and another very good friend, cheerful and kind, and we couldn't ask for more, had agreed to do the nursing checks on Tina at the uncare home. Helen had spent a long time there doing the ground work for the 'Friday meeting', which seemed to go well and that day finished on a high.... thank you Helen and Mandy. I was not called the rudest person that someone had ever met, but I am not sure if all we had agreed on would be carried out, but wait and see.

I was told that before the personal budget could be battled over we had to make sure that Tina could get high rate SDA*, and a solicitor must be seen to see if we could get some vestige of Enduring Power of Attorney. I had reservations about this as Tina, sadly, had no understanding, and legally she had to be able to say that she agreed to me being in charge

* Louise filled in the form but the high rate of SDA was dropped some time after Tina had received hers. A way of saving money?

of her allowances. I had to fill in a form for personal budget that did not seem to relate to Tina's situation. However we were told not to worry about the 'Power of Attorney' issue as Tina did not have very much money and after her funeral there wouldn't be anything left. Oh and if I die before Tina then one of her sisters will take my place without going through all the rigmarole. It doesn't seem normal to speak of these issues to a third party, but I suppose to a solicitor it is part of their working day. Each to their own.

The diggers were back cheerful as ever, Les our gardener was back and Pip from over the road. Spencer dug the gully to link up with the sewage system, the conifer too near to the Hut was dug out, the boiler had to be moved from the inside of the hut and a new one fixed outside, as it would not have been healthy near a sleeping Tina! It was so comforting to have people in the know who could help with these decisions.

We had been visiting Tina whilst all this work and decision making was happening. I recorded on one day that Tina was in a very happy state and even stood by pushing herself up on the chair arms. The 'bottom end' issue seemed sorted and she was to have just one sachet of Movacol every other day.

Quickly now, the drains are finished, the Baco Compac skip collected - some mutterings re the size of the load – and the lorry made it up the drive, now hugely empty but soon to have cars belonging to carers in it.

I went to see Tina in the afternoon, and she was so pleased to see me. The Movacol is working well for her. Auntie Janet had been to see her, who said Tina seemed very cheerful as she was being stimulated by Janet talking and massaging and creaming her legs. Janet lived very near to the home, her son is deaf and also had a learning disability, but she would pop and see Tina when she could.

Back to The Hut, oh please don't moan, the electrician finished the first fix in the kitchen, which Spencer had built, I don't think that we had to pay VAT on some of our goods for the hut as it was to be used in a nursing capacity, and a plasterer is coming from Norwich, probably a pal of Spencer's. Then the wet room was built and the kitchen finished, and 'just like that', Tommy Cooper the comedian would have said, it's all coming together.

And after that I went to choir! Just to say that Tina had never approved of our choir because we weren't famous and we had not been on the television, but she could be bribed to come to a concert with the promise of the food in the interval, and knowing that she would see some of the people she hung around with at the Kingburger café.

By now Tina had had one stay in the hospital because of the seizure and on the last day of April we were awakened by a member of the staff to say that Tina had had a seizure at 6.20am, but was sleeping now. Because we were going for a short break in a couple of day's time, we hurriedly packed some things, went quickly to see Spencer on his birthday, and then drove to the Hollow. There was a paramedic car outside for Tina and she was taken to hospital with one of the carers and we followed in the car. Again it was on the MAU ward as she was not recovering and her blood pressure was too low.

I rushed back home for the essentials I would need for my stay in MAU and when I returned Tina had been diagnosed with aspiration pneumonia - fluid leaking into the lungs. So that was it. No trip and no more back to the Hollow. Our lives will be totally involved with Tina's recovery and bringing her home. Page and Moy the travel company, were very sympathetic and offered a later date but from now on we could not make any plans except around Tina.

Tina and I are now on Stanhoe ward in a single room. I was offered a chair and a blanket but Louise found me a camp bed. So we were both quite comfortable and Tina was responding to the antibiotics, but still very vulnerable. She has been placed on an adult protection list.

The days are moving on. It is now voting day and Tina has always taken a great amount of interest especially if she sees David Cameron on the television. She has always used her vote which was her right, but not this time.

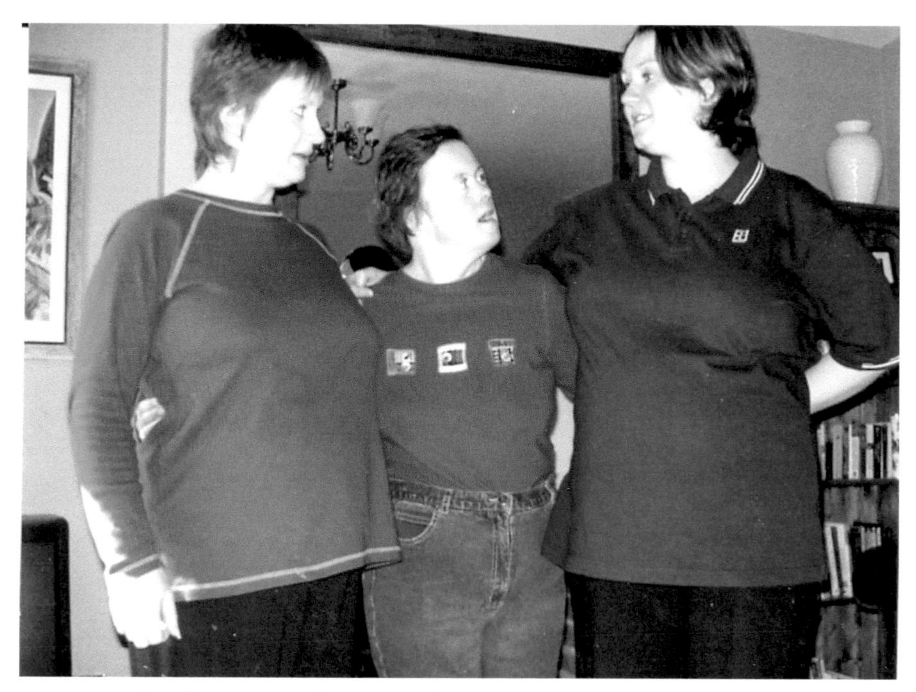

A lovely picture of Tina aged 43 with her two pregnant sisters.

Tina is looking very happy. She is with Sandra at one of her 50th birthday parties. Looking on is a young lady from Aspires, who helped people with learning difficulties.

We think the two ladies are Pat from 'Wuggerlands' and Jane is from Tom Thumb – they are still partying.

Come and Dance

Tina would like to invite

The World and his wife

to her 50th birthday party!

Saturday 18th October 2008

Great Massingham Village Hall

7.30 - 11.00 pm

Finger buffet   Bar available

Line Dancing with Yvonne, Rock Band Minority,

Card tricks with Matthew

Dress code: denims, checks, frills & boots!

RSVP by 10th October please

Phone Rachel - 01553 636644 NO PRESENTS REQUIRED

Email Louise - spencer@danielsbuildingservices.co.uk

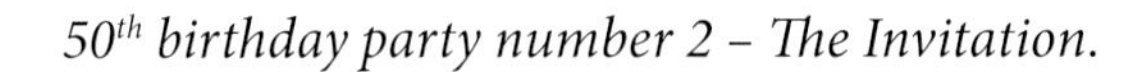

50th birthday party number 2 – The Invitation.

18

Tina Comes Home

Tina, and I, spent nine weeks in the hospital, following her multiple health issues starting with the seizure. Check out QE Visits in the Addenda to know the full story!* I was absolutely adamant that she was not going back to the uncare home, insisting that it had not been suitable for her needs. Now she was going to come home again to live in 'Tina's Hut' in the garden at Great Massingham, which had been skilfully adapted, and all we needed now were the carers. Our funding allowance was finally passed as appropriate giving us 24/7 care support at home.

Before our carers could start to come to work with us, the manager from Able came to make sure that her carers' sleeping arrangements were not in the same room as the patient, and that their food would be provided by us or they would be given money by us to buy and make their own. Their working day would start at 7.00am, with a 2 hour break around lunch time and then stay on duty until nine pm, when the night shift began. The manager was satisfied with the room, it also had an en suite which made for the carer's total privacy. She then asked me a question which I misunderstood as I thought that she had asked me 'would I like somebody back'.

I said if they would like to come back and if they had liked working with Tina then that would be fine. But no, I think she was asking if we would mind if someone was black. Oh dear, in fact the only one we found rather difficult was white. I suppose she was just doing her job asking this question.

---

* See addenda items QE Hospital visits and Case Conference Report

So moving on, Tina will be coming out of the hospital and the first carer will be coming the same day. Not all the way from Zimbabwe, the majority of the carers originated from there, because this carer had a client who lived locally, she worked between Tina and an elderly lady.

It was rather strange for all of us. Tina was coming back to live in her home, how we had all longed for this moment. It was very emotional as every time a different family member came it would be laughter and tears all over again.

Kumbie our new lady seemed to settle very quickly and she was very willing to learn how to use the hoist which was essential. I really valued my time in the hospital with Tina as I had learned by watching the nurses the best and correct way to move her from one position to another, with a slip sheet underneath to prevent her skin becoming damaged. This had to be done when her pad needed changing, meal times when she must be as upright as possible and then in a sloping position for relaxing perhaps sleeping and looking, hopefully in a pleasant way, at her visitors. These manoeuvres had at all times to be carried out by two people. Some carers were happy for me to be the 2nd, but others wanted to wait until another carer came and I always respected their decision. So this was the rule at our house also. Always two people now to wash, shower, dress and make sure that she is washed between every pad change.

At times some days seemed problematic but eventually everything was ironed out. That is me trying to make a joke as Kumbie absolutely loved ironing, so not only Tina's but all our clothes plus bedding were given her treatment. I made Tina's meals which had to be pureed and stored in the freezer until needed. We were beginning to establish new routines. Tony had taken on the role of head cook and he soon became more confident. The carers who had opted to cook their own meals soon changed their mind when they saw what was on offer. The meals mostly consisted of stewed meat mainly beef either in a pie, with dumplings, or curried.

Tony has insisted that he didn't use beef, only chicken. Carrying on and begging to differ.

At our tea time Tina would be brought over in her chair and sit with us, having already had her food. Sometimes she would laugh especially if someone started to sing and so she did seem to enjoy the atmosphere.

After tea we would relieve the carer of her responsibility and sit in the lounge with Tina which was nice for us all. Of course East Enders would be on if it was those days. I am not sure if Tina was recognising it now.

I don't think we were recognised either, but, one day when I was tidying up in the bathroom, I suddenly heard the word, Mum, in her voice! Or the voice that she had before this cruel illness took over her life.

I rushed into the room and said "Tina you said mum" but the moment had passed and she had taken on her vacant stare again, but at least I had heard it. The carers were pleased for me.

After Kumbie's week had passed and she had gone back to King's Lynn, I knew that we would miss her, but what about her family back at home in Zimbabwe, she had four children two boys and twin girls? Her husband taught at the university and she had been a midwife. I just thought it was so sad that she had to leave her family and come so far away from them to work - she telephoned them constantly often trying to find a bit of high ground to get a signal for her phone. After we had finished eating, Kumbie would relax in her room, or sometimes joined us. Then a local person from an agency in King's Lynn would come for the night shift and the two would work together to make Tina clean and comfortable for her nights sleep.

So that was our daily routine with different people of course and I must introduce Nancy to you. She lived very close to our house and offered to come some evenings to help in getting Tina ready for bed. I did wonder if she would be able to help with changing pads and cleaning Tina but I need not have worried. The first day while Tina was still in our lounge had what could be called an explosion! Nancy helped to clean up without any sign of revulsion and I knew that she would be an asset to our group, and she was, bright and cheerful and she often brought cake or biscuits which she had just taken out of the oven. We all looked forward to her coming.

Back to the African carers, some of their stories will stay forever in my mind. One, I will call her Lisa, was a fragile young lady and I did wonder if she would be suitable for moving Tina about, even with another person but she did. She always seemed permanently tired but when asked as to was her bed comfortable and did she sleep well she always replied in the affirmative. Then one day she spoke about her family. Her mother was a nurse and she had both an older and a younger brother living in England, and mum was working in a hospital here. I asked if her dad was still living in Zimbabwe,

"No, he died" was the answer to that.

I said that I was very sorry to hear that and more or less asked what had been the matter with him.

"He was not ill he had a car accident. The brakes had been tampered with, it was not an accident he had been killed." He supported the opposition in Zimbabwe and was quite outspoken in his mistrust of Mugabe so had to be got rid of. I was quite shaken to hear this and felt that maybe I had been too inquisitive asking about their lives, however Lisa seemed relieved to have been able to speak about it. I made her a cup of tea, she managed a smile and as it was nearly Tina's lunch time, I asked if she would like me to give her her lunch so she could have a break.

"O thank you" she said, "that is kind. Shall I help you to change her first?" After that was completed she quietly left the room.

There were times when it was nice for me to be with Tina on my own. I spoke to her after she had finished eating, telling her what I had been doing and who we had seen when we went on our little walk earlier in the day, and about the new baby to be* Sometimes she would really look as if she was understanding who or what I was talking about, perhaps there would be a sigh or a shake of whatever she was holding in her hand and another time there would be blankness.

Another of Tina's carers, Sarah, was a very big and strong lady, she could manoeuvre Tina, as in straighten her in her chair, with no effort and in a way that was comfortable for Tina, because I was watching. Again we used to sit and talk around Tina's bed and when Tina's head started to nod we would make her more comfortable for sleeping. I wonder if Tina heard the story of Sarah's uncle who had been incarcerated with Nelson Mandela.

---

* Louise was pregnant again and Theo was born on the 22nd Jan at 36+ gestation, weighing just over 3 pounds. Mum, Dad and brother Will were with him constantly and he made very good progress.

There is a lovely photo of Theo propped next to Tina on her bed.

Sarah showed me a picture of him, and what should have been a tall middle aged, slender man, was actually a frail old man, with long thin limbs slumped in a chair. The photo had been taken just after his release from Robin Island, and Sarah told me that he had died shortly after this picture was taken. A happier story was that Sarah's mum was a close friend of Archbishop Tutu's wife and they would meet often and drink tea together.

One night it was getting a little past Tina's time for being taken from the house to The Hut for her bedtime, requiring the night carer and Sarah to wash and change Tina in the hoist, so she could be transferred to the bed. Oh dear the hoist seemed to have died on us! After us all trying to make it work, to no avail, I rang the hoist man and explained our position, it was a Saturday night, it was nearly ten o clock and Tina was getting irritable. The man said that he would be with us asap. And he was. It was as if an angel had descended on us!

Whilst he was busy, we were relieved into silence except for Sarah who was still trying to amuse Tina. Suddenly the man paused and said "I hear your accent young lady where are you from?" I thought he can't be speaking to me but he was looking at Sarah. She answered him in a very cheery way and they both realised that they came from the same district, and they had a good old natter whilst he was fixing the hoist. I was relieved when it was repaired and Tina could be put into her bed, and I was so pleased to witness the ease of conversation between a black woman and a white man. Were we now really seeing progress now in South Africa?

The hoist never broke down again.

One lady came all the way from Bristol, and before we had the chance to welcome her, she held up what looked to me like a dog's full poo bag and announced that it was her meal for tonight as she was a vegetarian. It didn't look very appetizing to me, so I told her that Tina was also a vegetarian and that we were able to cook something for her. She was shown into The Hut by the carer who was about to move on and then came back to us with Tina to have our tea. I am not sure what happened to the 'poo bag' as she always ate her meal with us, refusing vegetarian food.

One lady, we shall call her Celia, came with a collection of wigs for herself, which she alternated daily. One Saturday we were having a big party and she knew about this event and saved her best wig for the occasion. Fortunately Tina was enjoying the atmosphere and so we were all able to stay to the end. Celia would have been very disappointed to have to leave the party before everyone else had left, as I think she actually forgot that Tina had to come first.

I did think what an exhausting job this must have been. The majority of carers did not have their own transport so they had to rely on buses which sometimes did not turn up. One lady who had to catch two buses came looking absolutely exhausted and shouted at me for not making her bed. I had been told not to as the new person had to see that the mattress had not been damaged. She was still not happy so I said that now she was here I would help her, she agreed and when she had recovered was a very good carer.

Gradually though the number of these carers seemed to be diminishing, probably because Tina was not an easy option and I suppose if they had the chance of an easier client they would choose the other one. Some people were going back to their homelands, Sarah was going back to Zimbabwe to marry someone from South Africa, and they would converse in English as neither could speak each others language! I do think of them and wish the best of lives for them all.

Our carers were now coming from a company called Allied based in King's Lynn, daytime workers and the night workers were the same, and if an extra person was needed during the night, it would be me, and perhaps Tony, for a back up.

These carers soon became familiar with Tina and what she needed, the GP visited on a regular basis whenever Tina had a seizure to check her medication and the speech and language therapist came to check that Tina was being given the correct food, at the correct temperature and sitting in the correct position. She was usually satisfied with what she saw, although Tina at times would not want her usual quantity so it had to be disposed of and not kept for the next meal time. All this would be logged on her sheet, and the carers were excellent with their record keeping so unlike the ones from the uncare home. But that is in the past.

Tina had a wheel chair which had been designed for her as soon as she came out of the hospital so on good weather days we could go out with her. She could only cope with this for a short time as she needed to change position, and because she was so well known we were constantly stopped for someone to greet her. On Wednesday afternoon it was tea/coffee and cake in church, and I could see that some people who had not seen Tina for a while were not sure what to say, and I really wanted to say to them 'it is still Tina and you can speak to her', especially to the ladies she used to chat to whilst waiting for her bus. Karen came to the rescue, she is very well known in the village and has a loud clear voice.

'Hello Tina don't you look well and that is a posh chair you've come in."

Well that broke the ice and I could see the bus ladies relaxing and smiling at Tina. When they left the church they all said goodbye to her, one lady kissed her, and after that tentative initial beginning they started to accept that Tina was where she was now in her life. Well done Karen.

Another weekly event to which I was invited to take her, was to Sing Your Heart Out or SYHO in short. I had been telling a friend about the looks of disapproval that we were being given when Tina started to shout loudly, she sadly had no speech now, when we were in the supermarket, or if we had ventured to another activity that we could watch. So Helen B invited us to go to the singing sessions which were held weekly. I was worried that it would spoil the session as SYHO was for people with a mental illness and singing can be a wonderful relief, but Helen assured me that the others would not mind, so we went to give it a try.

The people were so welcoming, moving chairs so that Tina plus chair could be at the front. Remember what Tina thought of singing groups.... CRAP, but at least, sadly, she wouldn't be shouting that out. I was a bit nervous, however it all went very well and we decided that we would try and go every week. When I said try and go... sometimes we would just run out of time, perhaps Tina had had a longer sleep than usual, she needed to have her lunch, she needed changing, think back to when you were taking a baby or toddler out, you are all ready to go and then....the same with Tina sadly, we would have to miss a week.

When we did go back again we were greeted very warmly and I think actually we had been missed. One week we were beating time with the singing and Tina had been given a shaker to rattle and she did just that, and carried on after the singing. She was really enjoying herself in her 'new Tina' way. We would take a snack for her as there was a pause in the singing and tea and biscuits were handed out, then we would start again. A very pleasant afternoon for us all.

Do you remember the Gateway club? Of course you do. Every alternate Monday evening. We would do our best to get there. The club members, or at least the people who knew Tina did immediately come and speak to her, however they found it difficult to understand why she couldn't talk to them anymore. I just said that she was poorly now but that she was pleased to be here. So we just sat quietly and watched. This was difficult for me.

The red van bought specifically to transport Tina could be temperamental. The mechanism that would allow the wheelchair and Tina to be lowered to the ground was operated by a switch, usually by the carer as she was sitting nearest to it. Well one day it did drop to let Tina out but then, worst nightmare, it would not go up. The carer took Tina into the club, and Tony really tried to get it to start again until the people started to leave. I had gone in periodically to see Tina and to up date. We had tried to contact the hoist people to no avail and the carer had got in touch with her manager to let our night man know the situation. We could have all had lifts back but not Tina in the wheel chair, then a breakthrough. A young lad said one of the taxis could take a wheel chair with Tina and the carer, and he had the card with a phone number on it. Hurrah! I phoned and fortunately he could come, what a relief and he was a very nice chap. Well done the young man who had the presence of mind to carry the card with the phone number in case he needed it. I must have bought him something! Again Everybody can do Something.

So they set off and Tony and I had to get in touch with the police and tell them that a red van was having to be left, fully open opposite the flats on the Fleet. We were told to take all the loose belongings with us and the police on duty would check to see if everything was as safe as it could be. I am not sure who took us home, and the van was repaired the next day.

That was the last time Tina went to the club as her condition was deteriorating.

It is 'World Cruise' time now. Tina had a wonderful experience with Ronnie the Dolphin. This is on Roatan Island in Honduras.

At Lou and Spen's wedding, seated are Lou, Spen and Will. Standing from left are Spen's mother Diane and his brother, Tina and Josette.

At Lou and Spen's wedding are best friends Audrey and Alan with Tina of course.

19

Christmas 2011

21st December

'It's coming on Christmas
Cutting down trees
Putting up reindeer
Singing songs of joy and peace'

(apologies to Joni Mitchell)

Prior to the preparations for Christmas 2011 in the little hut, there had been activity in the kitchen of the house. Two small pots of food had already been carefully labelled 'Christmas Surprise', and then put into the freezer to await the big day.

What secrets were the pots carefully guarding? Think hard now. Yes it must have been a chocolate sponge pudding with custard to make the correct consistency. Neither too thick, causing immediate choking nor too thin which would slip into her lungs too quickly, it's the dysphagia you see. In the other pot there must have been cheese and potato pie. Not very Christmassy but think vegetarian, her choice which was always adhered to, with regard to her swallowing disorder which required every morsel or drink to have to be so smooth, so that from a tiny plastic spoon this morsel could be placed into her mouth, and slide down the oesophagus without entering the lungs.

This preparation was completed before the drug driver was attached to her thigh. Because when this had taken place hardly anything else went in to be ingested, or most likely choked over, most definitely not a Christmas surprise.

A countdown game is being played out now. As the doctor said in the practical way that doctors have when a piece of knowledge has to be passed from themselves to the patient's family, making sure that they understand there is no going back now.

Understood.

The heart shaped plaque, 'Tina's Hut' it called itself, fixed to the wall near to the door where it could be seen by all who entered, was dazzling with the artistic carer's careful arranging of silver garlands and baubles which caught the light. There were two small trees inside with their ever changing lights.

"Don't put them on the fast mode it will aggravate her eyes." said the mother when she came in that morning.

It was the 11th day of the drug driver in situ and it was slowly and relentlessly travelling with Tina towards the inevitable end.

There were cards balanced on ledges, these had been sent personally to Tina. Every card wished for her at the least a happy Christmas and then joyous, magical, wonderful, fun, love, hugs were thrown into the mix, written with the emphasis at times of capital letters, willing her to enjoy one more Christmas. It was a big ask.

Her baby sister had sent her heart, with two pompoms, into her card and ended with Tina's names for them all 'Wlice, Espencer, Wonky, licky nephew and down dog.'

There was a Rudolph, a Robin, fat Teddy, cold snowman, a carefully coloured in mum and baby, they were there to bring their joys and peace to a worn out little lady.

There were carols and Christmas disco songs to be played. Tina wasn't too fussed about carols,

'D'you'ave to', she would complain when the mother started to sing, she was old Tina then of course.

In her prime she would dance away, rock and roll with Sheila, twist again, dancers would pause and watch, she loved it all.

All this reminiscence. Another of Tina's one liners,

'It's doing my head in' and it was. 'Don't think anymore just keep going,' was the mother's instruction to herself.

She sat on the chair which was placed so close to the bed that whoever sat there would smell the freshness of the linen, the gentle soap which was used on her skin and the sweet breath that was coming, very gently now out of her mouth. She breathed them all, drinking in all the sweetness - who could say if this was to be the last day of her daughter's life. She placed her cheek so gently on her daughter's cheek, only for a second because her body had begun to quiver under this oh so gentle touch. It was too much. She managed to choke her usual 'see you later' to the carer and left the room.

22nd December

It had been one of many sleep deprived nights for the mum and the best mate. Today baby sister and June and Jamie were coming. Tina was propped in her usual position for comfort but her face had developed a pallid look which was not apparent yesterday. They sat talking quietly taking turns to hold her hand. The visitors said their goodbyes and then the mother just appeared to need some air and announced that she was going to plant the cyclamens. 'Sunday Morning Jeanne' and her just pregnant daughter came, so the wild idea that she wanted to escape from the inevitable was put to one side. It was agreed that Tina looked different and the nurse was called. It was the 12th day of the drug driver.

The baby sister was told the news that Tina was beginning her final journey as she arrived back at her home, and so she turned around and came back. The dignified sister came, wondering if she could give her children their tea. Probably not. The best mate wanted to make food for everyone but nobody was in the mood, so he showed the carer pictures of his grand parents, in the house. The carer apologised but she was needed there, occupying a man who did not want to accept the inevitable, that he was about to lose his very dear friend and they, the mum and the two sisters sat together holding onto the tired little person who had given them so much joy, laughter, love and frustration, for all the sisters lives and most of the mother's. The nurse who was so professional discreetly kept a very low profile. They attempted singing quietly and then lapsed into silence. Glances were passed between themselves and the clock. At a few moments before 7.00pm Tina's last breath came. Very, very peaceful and the mother could hear as if so far away the sobbing of her daughters and yes from the nurse as well. It was as if she was not a part of it, she was the onlooker from far away. And she didn't know when her daughters left and were they safe to drive. And the best mate coming and sobbing his goodbye to his friend and ally, the good friend who helped the carers at night, the changing and washing of Tina (carer taking the bedding to wash), the sadness of another neighbour, and then suddenly Tina and her mother were on their own as they had been the night she was born just over 53 years ago. Just the two of them for the last time.

And then the undertakers came,

"She isn't going in a bag" she shouted and,

"Yes I am staying here until you have taken her. I am alright on my own, I prefer it."

And then she was gone with the two strangers, the mother watching, not waving as was her custom.

She locked the door and went into the house leaving the hollow reminder of a Christmas that wasn't going to happen because the main character in this final scene, like a premature Father Christmas, had just left the building. Leaving behind not only a fragmented family who had gone to their respective homes, but also the joy, peace, love and whatever else was written in all the cards balancing on the ledges in Tina's hut.

Decisions – leaving 'Wuggerlands' care home after twenty-eight years. Pat is helping Tina to cut her cake. Looking on is Carol the manager.

Addendum

These are my observations of when my daughter Tina was treated as an in-patient in the QE. There are 5 visits, the last with a duration of 9 weeks.

The incidents which I will cover will show a deterioration of Tina's ability and how the staff coped with both Tina and myself.

1st visit

The year was 1998, she was in her fortieth year and before the onset of her dementia.

1.Varicose veins stripping of: was admitted to a surgical ward day before and almost managed to answer by herself all the questions concerning her state of health, routines i.e. washing, dressing, showers food etc. although I was there to assist with translating as Tina's speech was not always clear. I went home at the end of visiting hours knowing that she knew where the toilet was in the ward, she would be given a meal for her vegetarian requirements and I would return before she was taken to the theatre. The nurse did ask if she would be alright and I had no hesitation in saying that she would be and I would be back asap the next day.

The experience and the outcome of the procedure were good.

2nd visit

In 2007 Tina was admitted to a surgical ward to have a cataract removed under general anaesthetic, and was put into a side room. Tina's ability (she was moving much nearer to being given the diagnosis of dementia) had decreased substantially and therefore it was impossible for her to stay there unaided. There was no possibility that she would be able to communicate with the staff. The staff were happy for me to stay and my daughter asked if I could have some bedding for the chair. One thing I remember was that the door was always closed firmly whenever a member of staff left the room. I had asked for it to be left open each time but that was ignored. So I would open it as I felt we needed to be part of the hospital environment. And so the ritual proceeded, nurse left the room, door closed, I opened it, nurse passing by closed it. No one answered my question why is the door being closed. Was Tina supposed to have something contagious? After a restless night for both of us I had to forget the door. Poor communication. Drops had to be administered before the op. If she had been 'old Tina', she would have tolerated this but she was 'new Tina' now, didn't understand so shouted loudly. Nurse left the room and I had to manage unaided.

After the op she was very distressed and kept attempting to pull off the eye patch. Nurse would peer around the door and hurriedly put the medication onto the first ledge she could find and hurry off. Could I ask who would have supported Tina during this? And who was supporting me to administer the drops which had to be given 4 times over 24 hours.

At this time in her life, although she was still ambulant, she needed support to walk to the toilet and she could feed herself but needed supervision. Ditto with drinks.

The op was a success although she was very distressed, but the pre and post care were not supportive. This seemed to be discrimination; the only time she seemed to be a human being was when a nurse / sister came on duty who recognised Tina from where we had lived and spoke very warmly to her and then everyone else did the same. Remarkable. I wish she had been on duty earlier.

So outcome good, service patchy and poor communication if the staff thought that Tina was in a side room for a sinister reason and not discuss the issue with me.

One show of support for myself was a dinner lady offering me a dinner she had left on the trolley - with the proviso of not to tell anyone or she would get the sack. Being sacked for giving a tired, hungry mother a leftover dinner, what next?

3rd visit

Moving on to 2009 and Tina was to be taken to A and E following a tonic clonic seizure. I could not prevent her falling and banging her head on a radiator. I followed previously given instructions that if an injury occurred during a seizure the patient must be seen by a paramedic and possibly taken to hospital.

She began to regain consciousness, the ambulance arrived, the wound was bleeding and the area around the eye was beginning to swell. The ambulance men looked at Tina then us but did not seem to be in a hurry to put her on a stretcher. One went back to the ambulance and brought a chair. It appeared not to be their job to lift someone or was it discrimination? My husband has MS and heart trouble and I was slighter than Tina, so between us we could not lift her onto either a stretcher or a chair. They helped, grudgingly it seemed. Discrimination?

In the hospital, on a bank holiday Saturday. A&E did not seem to be very busy but the mood was sullen. I thought naively she would be given an X-ray or at least someone to look at her eye and in a more thorough way than a cursory look and wander off without an explanation. Can she have pain killers? Apparently not. The wound was still bleeding and Tina needed to go to the toilet. Nurse made a comment about it being too late. Correct but where was the offer of finding pads or pants?

(Just a general point here, a huge concern to patients in a side room, ward or trolley is to be able to get to a toilet. And people cannot hang on especially when they are old or disabled.)

Tina was finally given butterfly stitches, no x ray of course, it was the weekend and to the staff it was not essential but seizures were a new concept to us at this time in Tina's life and I needed an assurance that in the opinion of a qualified person we could leave and she would recover.

It sounds mean but that day I gave the service including ambulance 1 out of 10, if that.

Another point on behaviour, being at work should not include personal chat especially loud voices shouting across the department.

Just to add a P.S. to this account which has nothing to do with the hospital, ---.In the afternoon of that day Tina was looking more cheerful so we decided to go to Snettisham where we were supposed to be going because it was the Norton Hill Miniature Railway day and our Mencap were providing the refreshments. (keeping the money that was made for our funds.)

A chair was found for Tina and the story of her falling after the seizure, the wound on her head, the unhelpful ambulance men and the uninterested hospital staff became the focal point of the afternoon, well after the railway rides of course. She did start to look more cheerful but she did not have a train ride on that day. Nor did she go to Wuggerlands until her wound was healing and then I took her in and picked her up. (It was the school holiday so I was not missing work.)

4th visit

2009 again. Our next incarceration was on MAU following a seizure. Tina was brought in by ambulance from the home where she was staying and that is another story.

We were in A and E for a long time but the attention, kindness and courtesy, as in treating her as a human being, were 8 out of 10's worth of points.

Onto MAU and into a side room. Blood on the toilet seat and on the floor. Cleaners coming next a.m. and use another toilet, and no medication brought in by the staff from the home. Good start. Next day on the main ward to await the review of Tina's meds. Her meds had to be ordered as they were now in liquid form, (thickened, dysphagia) and hers were at the 'uncare' home. She had been admitted following a seizure and no meds for 36 hours.

A nurse in charge asked if I was staying so I asked if there was anyone who would be able to look after her during the night, she had to tell me that no, there was nobody so she accepted my answer that I would stay.

How was she going to get to the toilet? A young nurse who really wanted to help said that she knew where there was a mobile hoist, but when she triumphantly brought it there was no sling and she did not know where there was one and nor did anyone else. I gave up.

Equipment must always be on every ward or at least staff should be aware of where it is in case it is needed.

My impression of that ward - crowded of course, noisy with shouting patients, trolleys backwards and forwards, lights on almost continuously, buzzers sounding, a hell hole indeed. Where did my sympathies lie? Staff or patients. Thinking about it today, 2016, I really don't know. But it is not the place for the vulnerable, sick, & bedridden who make up a large proportion of the community.

Dare I stick my neck out, all who are in a high authority within the hospital should spend a night in MAU, incognito of course.

5th visit

It is now 2010 and Tina will be in the hospital for 9 weeks from 30 April to the 6th or 7th July following her admittance with more seizures and aspirational pneumonia. She was suffering now with dysphagia and the staff at the 'uncare' home just kept running out of the thickener needed. And we could not bring it in!!

So this was the start of the 9 weeks.

On the ward, our new home to be. There was an isolation side room on that ward which we were eventually able to move into when the patient had left. And I presume no one else needing to be in isolation. Whilst on this ward we moved to three different side rooms and I moved from chair to mattress to bed and back to mattress.

The staff were concerned about these arrangements but it was all 'doable' with myself, family and friends taking turns to Tina sit, on a 24/7 rota.

One incident which put Tina onto her second police protection of a vulnerable adult

1st was the lack of thickener in drinks, the 2nd was on finding by 2 staff nurses, who were catheterising Tina, large red bruises inside her vaginal area. They looked very shocked and asked if I had seen these which I had not.

Doctor called next day to examine, stood at the end of the bed, said he did not need to examine as nurses had already examined. Nurse looked embarrassed.

I said someone should, following police and social services involvement.

GUM clinic would not. Not their responsibility.

Gynaecology also refused, at first.

A friend, Helen arrived and issued an ultimatum to a very young doctor. 'Show me where the gynae dr's car is and I will sit by it until he leaves.'

Now Tina had been summoned to see the gynae dr. Result? I could not be sure. Eventually settled for poor care.

Was this a case of discrimination? Male doctors refusing to examine a vulnerable female patient.

She had an outpatient app. Could the dr. come to the ward? He never did.

Treatment by staff did vary. The consultants were cold and indifferent. Apart from Mr J.

The more experienced nurses were relaxed, kind and thorough.

Some assistants were similar and were very grateful for me to double up with them as in toileting, washing and of course feeding. One 'green' nurse marched off to the kitchen and said that I must be allowed to fill in a sheet for at least one meal a day and the cleaning lady told me where I could buy a snack very near to the ward. I thought it was for staff as I had seen white coats in there.

Others were unwelcoming to me, unsure of how to use the sling and hoist and wanted to be off as soon as it was break time.

You have to be thick skinned.

If someone was visiting then between us we could do everything for Tina and the staff who were confident could see the sense of it. I felt I was there because my daughter could not be discharged until her room at our house was ready, and we had the budget to care for her at home. She was not going back to the 'uncare' home. I am sure social services compensated the NHS.

It was a very difficult time for all of my family, however the majority of staff on the ward could see the sense of someone staying with her at all times. I really hope that this experience should be extended to all families who find themselves in a similar situation to our own. I know that my daughter's needs could not have been met without 1 to 1, 24/7. I look back on it all now with relief as to what had been achieved. One rather amusing story before we conclude was one day our friends June with her son Jamie, and Sue were Tina sitting but Tina was not in a happy mood and I did not like to leave them until she was settled. We started to sing a song that Tina liked but that did not work as she suddenly shouted out 'Bloody Hell'. We paused all of us including Tina and then we burst out laughing.

She soon settled after that. I collected some of my clothes, went home for a shower and was back for the night shift. I slept four nights, Mandy, you remember from Mencap, slept two and sister Rachel one. Louise would visit as many days as she could including weekends with Spen and Will, just making sure that everything was going to plan. Helen also on her visits made sure that everything was going to plan, and never left if she hadn't got the answers she wanted. One night she decided that I needed a break and her, dare I say long suffering cousin, was called in to stay the night. Not quite what she expected and the nurse who was trying to help had never met Tina before. They muddled through which I thought was admirable.

I did wonder if the story I had heard, was that at one time Tina was in the Queen's room. I did not believe this but if the Queen was in need of surgery at any time when she, for example was at Sandringham, then this would be in the general hospital and not in the private one which was next door with a connecting internal passage. What does a reader think to that. It did seem larger than the other rooms we had been in.

To conclude My Advice

If you are vulnerable then you need an advocate to be your voice and what better than someone in your family. Please encourage and expect family to be in the ward, especially at meal times and suggest that toileting & washing could be done by them at all times. Do not let the fear of being in the way stop the daily routines. Please always consult with family as to the patient's needs. It was a learning curve for all our family and thanks to the nurses who showed us how to use the hoist and sling, to sit or lie Tina in the best positions and to slide (up the bed) WITH A SHEET.

I missed the nurses. It was like taking a new baby home.

Yes, a new baby how good that will be for Lou , Spen and Will.

Still keeping to 'how Tina was treated' this next piece of information came from Louise, who many times after Will had gone to school, would drive over to the uncare home and stay with Tina until she had to get back at the end of the school day.

One day this is what she found. The words are hers.

On arrival at 10.20am two very inexperienced staff were on duty (one was the gardener). They were concerned as to Tina,s condition but were unsure of what to do to support her. Within seconds I had identified that she was too hot and needed fluids, her mouth was very dry. She also needed sitting up. Whilst one member of staff agreed she had too many layers on, she had been in bed for three hours becoming dehydrated and over heated. Within forty five minutes Tina had drank 600m of thickened squash. I asked one of the staff to take Tina's temperature as I could hear that her chest was 'rattly'. He did not know the whereabouts of the thermometer and did not know how to open the meds cabinet. I asked him to contact ? who was on call, she didn't answer. Eventually the thermometer was found and I took Tina's temperature, the person on duty said he had never used it before so handed it to me! Whilst the staff were very pleasant their inexperience was apparent so I felt in overall control of Tina's needs. A senior member of staff made contact but it was not ?

My main concern is had I not have visited with the thickener Tina would have received drinks again without it, making her chest even more rattly. It was the responsibility of senior staff to make sure that there was always a back up of this substance and there were no seniors on duty that day.

Why one might ask. This had happened before, the staff on duty made a big show of looking for something that they knew that they did not have. Forgot again! The approach is too relaxed. Tina has a medical condition that states thickener is a necessity.

Lack of pads is a huge concern. Mum was informed of this and left money for pads to be bought. They never were. My husband on Sunday evening visited five chemists trying to purchase them. Everything was left until the last moment, they were supposed to be supporting vulnerable people.

There were times when Tina's meds were not recorded. Some staff do (record) some don't. Not a good policy. How do they know if she has taken them or not.

To conclude this part of the document. A huge shake up is necessary or there may be an untimely death.

I feel that an example of how the residents reacted with each other should be told. One day Tony (best mate) and I were visiting Tina and so on entering the room we found her sitting with J. who she did know reasonably well. I called out a greeting, Tina turned to look at me and to my horror I saw that her face had red patches on it , one very near to her eye. There was the sound of laughter coming from the kitchen where the staff had gathered so I knocked on the door and it was opened by someone feigning surprise. As in ' oh didn't know you were here'. I pointed to Tina's face in a silent way and waited for an explanation. Nothing came. Why were they sitting in a separate room putting Tina and J. together when (we were told that J had turned against Tina) and nobody with them! I was so angry saying to Tony that He was right and she was not going to stay there.

You will have read earlier in the book how we began to make this happen in the earlier part of this story.

The whole attitude was faulty. Eg, Tina had an appointment at the hospital and it was arranged for me to meet, Tina, the manager and her sidekick at the hospital. When I got there to the designated place which was at this time in a busy corridor I saw Tina's chair with Tina in it, but nobody else. Of course Tina couldn't tell me anything so I just stayed with her with my hand on her arm and we waited. The two carers, one being the manager, came sauntering out of the toilet and seemed surprised to see me. They had both been in the toilet together leaving Tina unaccompanied, in a busy place. She should never have been left alone, what if she had had a seizure. They were acting like school girls having a day out. The time for her returning could not come soon enough.

PS. Yes she did come home. Everything was ready for her in 'the hut' and her first carer was ready and waiting. We all had some lovely times together until finally her body could take no more. She died peacefully on the twenty second of December. The year was 2011.

Life and Times with Tina

Tina is the eldest of the five children born to her dad and me. Tina and I have been together for 49 years and shared many happy and sad times. The births of her siblings, mine and Tony's marriage, the births of Will Claire and Ed (my grandchildren) being the happiest, and the deaths of very precious family members being the worst. In between these two extremes, and despite her start in a hostile environment (the doctor told her dad 'best to put her away', 'and have another child soon'), Tina became very confident, happy, friendly, cheerful and loving. She always showed an independence of spirit, of which I thoroughly approved, and was an integral part of the family, even though everything did not always go smoothly. The same must be true of all families surely?

After attending Alderman Jackson School and the Adult Training Centre, (Remember the professional who came to the house to decide which would be the best place for Tina to complete her education?) so Tina gained independence and freedom. She was able to use buses on her own, undertook college courses, did voluntary work at a local home for the elderly for 28 years, learnt to swim really well (mostly underwater), had great holidays with family and other groups and loved being with people and finding out all about them. She made deep, close friendships, and many people gained enormous pleasure from her company and personality. She loved to dance, the twist was her favourite, and was the life and soul of any party. She celebrated her major birthdays in style, a country and western group at her 18th, the surprise party at the Blue and Gold, and discos at the rest. She gave a wonderful speech at her 40th, and a lovely comment on a card from the 49th/50th cappuccino party said that 'when Tina walks in the room, it lights up.'

Tina was very determined and caring. She went with me to see her dad when he was ill in hospital, but after he died she took herself to see him at the undertakers without discussing it with me or seeking any help. Similarly, when she was determined to see her sister in hospital, who was waiting for her Caesarian, she found her way to the correct maternity ward, again without telling any of us and without help.

Her strong personality showed when she announced she had become vegetarian, which she stuck to thereafter, and declared herself a Conservative voter, with an especial attraction to David Cameron. She preferred to do things independently, e.g. she liked to vote on her own, sit apart from myself on buses, visit friends and take refreshments in her favourite cafes, despite the occasional hiccup e.g. taking the wrong bus, leaving her handbag on the cafe table from where it was stolen!

Tina liked country & western music, particularly Martine McCutcheon and Tony Christie, he was always with us in the car. When the wrestlers came to King's Lynn Tina was always in attendance and sat as near as she could to the ring. When there was someone she knew there who was as big a fan as she was, they would cheer for their favourites. I would arrive back at the allotted time and stand and watch her loving it. Each to their own I say!

Tina could do 1000 piece jigsaws, she knitted blankets for her niece and nephews, made cakes, she walked up Snowden, and took part in a swimathon for cancer research,

"For my dad" she said.

Tina met Darren at the Gateway club and he really was the love of her life, what a charmer but what a con! He was seeing 3 other women at the time and it all ended in tears and was very hard for her. The next man she fell for was Spikey Mike at the playgroup where she also volunteered, and thankfully he was mature enough to handle her with care, and she always referred to his partner as his 'ex-wife'.

So Tina has experienced all human emotions and had a full and very active 'working' life and I always felt that she was a marvellous advocate for herself and for her condition and I have felt privileged to belong to, as we refer to it, the club.

This is all very positive but there were increasing signs of difference in Tina's abilities and personality. Tina had always been clumsy and rough but now even more so. Remember the 'thick glove' test? This helped me to understand her increasing difficulties in opening delicate objects and how her CD player got 'Knackered', so she had to listen through the computer. She continued to love wrestling, but now watching it on TV every Sunday before visiting 'Sunday morning Jeanne and Ant.'

Tina now looked uncomfortable on the dance floor, slow moving and sitting down at the first opportunity; was isolating herself more; losing/misplacing her hat, gloves, purse, bus pass etc; poor time-keeping; putting clothes on inside out; her writing skills disappeared. Re-assessment by Phil at the Park View Resource Centre confirmed her slide into dementia and she was put on medication.

We had to accept another bereavement in our family. Our old Tina gradually disappeared and in her place was a demanding anxious, irritable, rude Tina, confused at times unless in a strict routine, and not as nice! During this period our lives continued, dipped, recovered and then slid ominously downwards. Tina's ability seemed to see-saw between being old Tina & the new Tina, irritable, anxious to be at home and confused about what day it was.

Tina was now spending 4 days a week at Aspires, not doing a lot but happy to go, and taking a squeaky duck to tease them with. Two other days were spent at Involve, which she liked because she was taken to buy her TV times. Taken? Tina was once quite capable of picking up shopping in Sainsbury's for us but she is new Tina now. Tom Thumb play group didn't want to lose her so on some Fridays I took her to visit. At the weekends she was with us, but now watched more carefully-she still visited her friends & neighbours on Sunday morning after the wrestling and went to the shop, but that was the extent of her unsupported life. I wondered sometimes what she thought about it, when one day she suddenly said ' it's my memory isn't it?'

One happy thing for me was that Tina was enjoying respite care which was a great relief to us because we did need respite as her time with us could be quite draining. Because we could not leave her alone anymore she had to be bribed with a cappuccino to accompany us. Shopping was always halted for visits to the toilet, but we had got used to all this, and when Tina suddenly announced that she was glad she came, then we are so pleased. That cannot be guaranteed - nothing can anymore. One thing I feel saddened about is that when Tina is being difficult when we are out I am sure that onlookers will think it is the Downs syndrome.

Dementia is cruel to all the family. I do not know how I would have managed without Tony to be in for Tina when she arrived home, and my girls taking her when they could. They were a wonderful support, as was our strong and pro-active Mencap group in Kings Lynn.

The Future was going to become bleaker as dementia does not go away and I was hoping that we would remain strong enough to cope. One absolute body blow to us was the threatened withdrawing/sacking of the psychiatric team, because just knowing that a professional was within easy reach was a comfort. We were in an unenviable position of the support being pulled from under our feet, and we felt we were now skating on the thinnest of ice. We may soon be drowning not waving!

Inexorably Tina's condition deteriorated, the anti-dementia drug was withdrawn and she was put on sodium valproate to counteract seizures, which turned into the clonic tonic type. Scary to start with and I don't think we will ever come to terms with them. She became very childlike ie always wanting to be the first, and getting upset. She was mega sensitive to touch and if she decided it was time to do something we all had to be ready. I discovered that it was easier to be slightly one step ahead, watch out for the first signs of Tina wanting to be on the move and not keep her waiting, if I showed her my coffee cup and said I had nearly finished, then she was more inclined to wait. The toilet was a major problem for Tina and myself, as she protested quite violently when she being cleaned up, so we needed to get a new style Closomat toilet, an all singing, all dancing loo and bidet.

This all sounds very doom and gloom but we did have a marvellous celebration. Not knowing what Tina's state of mind was going to be like when she reached 50, I thought it would be the right thing to do to celebrate a year early, so just after her 49th birthday we had a wonderful party at the Ffolkes Arms. Tina did seem rather phased and didn't recognise some people who were upset at this, but she was just waiting for her good mate Sandra to come, and she stuck like glue to her until people from Woodlands and the play group got her dancing. We called it a cappuccino party and requested people to wear something light and frothy. At the end of the night when we arrived back home Tina said 'mm nice party'. So I decided that it had been a good idea. However she kept reminding me that she would be 50 next!

And of course there was The World Cruise still to come!

But now I had all Tina's needs to care for; toileting; showering; hair wash/drying; dressing; pills breakfast; teeth; toilet bag; packing if it was an Aspires day; then some respite until 3.45pm and we started the afternoon/evening shift. In between we had to cram in washing; cleaning; bit of gardening; making doctors/dentist etc appointments; socialising; shopping; meetings; non Aspires days with Tina in tow, plus wipes and pants in my handbag. On non Aspires days something had to be planned to amuse Tina otherwise she had no focus with no hobbies to speak of except looking for the light, emptying the dish washer, whistling, talking about Sandra etc over and over, looking for her water bottle/tv times' and you can't fill a day like that - well you can when it's repeated over and over!

Tina and I are on our journey, some days are a struggle, some are pleasant and some are amusing. Tina still has the knack of her brilliant one liners.

One day in the George hotel, Tina must have been listening to a lady who was discussing something political with her friend, and she suddenly moved closer to the lady and said,

"I'm a Conservative too, y'know".

I didn't hear the lady's reply, we hurried out.

A few words of advice to the professionals. Parent carers are in a very fragile state and Tina was in an even greater one. If you are pro carer I hope you are working within a strong team because you also will need the support to help your clients.

If you are a politician - please don't keep coming up with new ideas. New ideas have a hollow ring and are usually only concerned with saving money and not in the patient's or their families best interests. We do live in the 4th richest nation in the world.

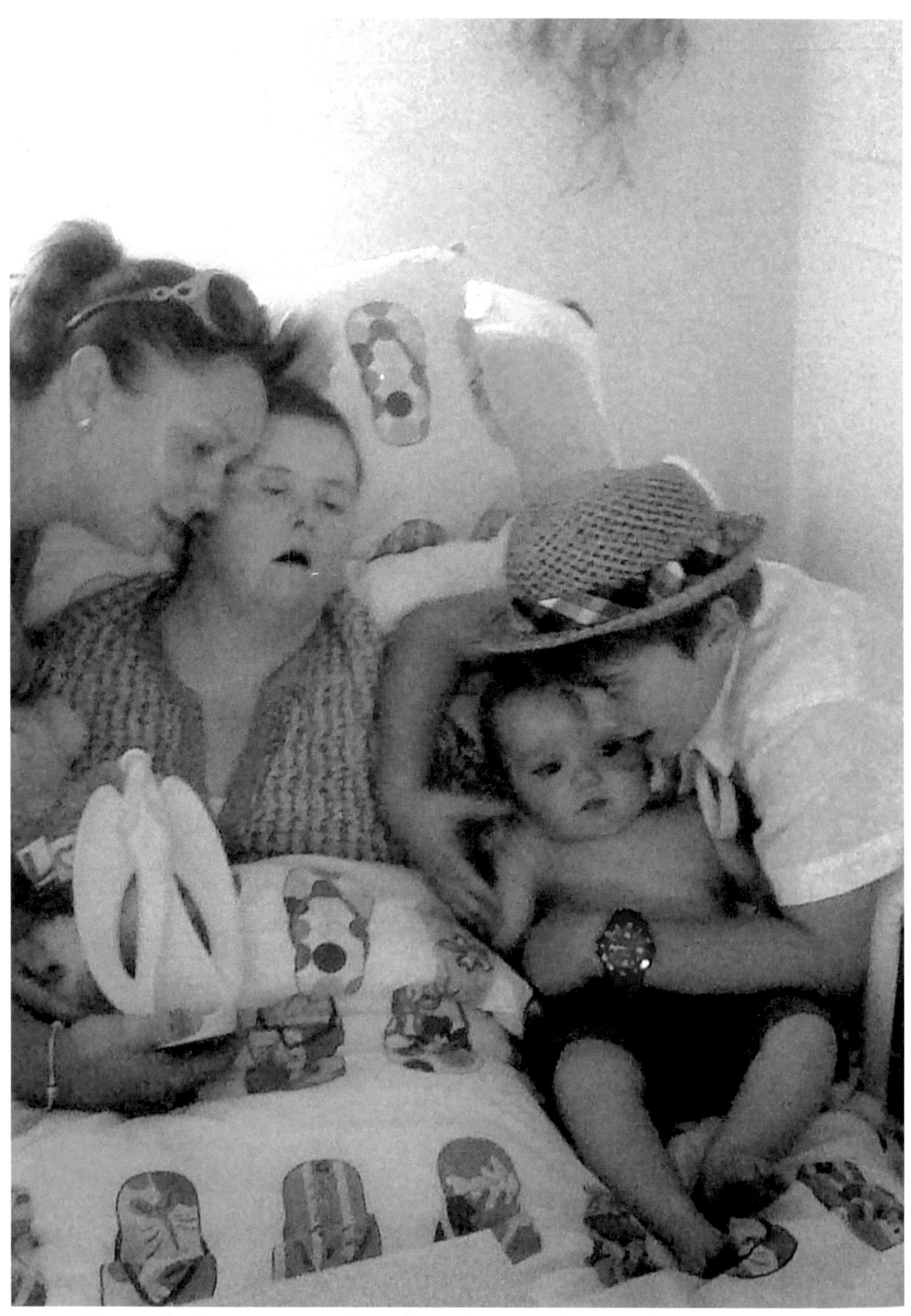

This is the last picture to be taken of Tina. She is with new baby Theo, Will and Lou.